# 40 YEARS OF BRITISH
# *Arab Horse Champions*

## 1953-1992

Compiled by Deirdre Hyde

ℋ

ALEXANDER HERIOT

Alexander Heriot & Co. Ltd
P.O. Box 1, Northleach
Cheltenham, Gloucestershire GL54 3JB
England

ISBN 0-906382-09-2

Typeset by Gilcott Graphics, Rushden, Northamptonshire
Printed and bound by Woolnough Bookbinding Ltd,
Irthlingborough, Northamptonshire

To
LILIAS MACVIE
FRIEND, MENTOR AND
INSTIGATOR OF MY PASSION
FOR THE ARAB HORSE

# ACKNOWLEDGEMENTS

This book would not have been possible without Gillian Lancaster, who very generously allowed me to make full use of her *Photonews* archive. I also owe a particular debt to the photographers Peter and Marilyn Sweet, Betty Finke, Fiona Guinness and Christine Massey for providing most of the later material. Their collections are the treasure troves of the future. In addition, Rosemary Archer kindly let me borrow photographs of two of the early horses in order to complete the sequence properly.

Finally, my whole-hearted thanks to Jane Kadri and Linda Churchill for their constant encouragement and assistance throughout the time it has taken me to compile this work.

# PREFACE

This book is a collection of photographs of the purebred in-hand Champions at the Arab Horse Society's annual Shows between 1953 and 1992. I would have liked also to include the ridden classes to illustrate that the Arabian has a function as well as being beautiful but, until recent years, the quality of available photographs was regrettably not adequate for publication in book form. I trust that I may be forgiven this omission.

Nevertheless, there should be much within these covers to appeal to breeders, owners and readers alike. We start when three of our most influential personalities were still to the fore: Lady Wentworth at the Crabbet Arabian Stud, Miss Gladys Yule at Hanstead and Bill Musgrave Clark at Courthouse. The years that followed saw the dispersal of Crabbet and Hanstead and that great surge of interest in the Arabian horse that has latterly led to the importation of many influential animals from Poland, Russia, Spain, the United States and several other countries.

It is invariably interesting and often educative to compare the Champions of today with those of yesteryear, to watch the pendulum of fashion at work, to assess the changes that are visible and to note the persistence of certain characteristics in generation after generation of some families. To be able to see a progression of what was judged the best in Britain over a span of 40 years is an absorbing experience and I hope also a welcome one to all admirers of the Arab horse.

A word about the principal source of photographs – a Mr and Mrs Spicer who traded under the name of *Photonews* and for many years were the only official photographers at the Shows. When I first attended one, at Kempton Park in 1964, they were probably at their peak and I am sure I speak for many others when I say that I quietly offer up a blessing for their truly indefatigable work which has created a record not only of the Champions but also of nearly every horse that was exhibited during their reign. By the same token, all credit to Gillian Lancaster who has taken upon herself the pleasant duty of preserving this unique archive. Her patience in dealing with my numerous requests was an example even to saints.

Deirdre Hyde
March 1993

# NOTES TO THE TEXT

For many years the in-hand purebred Championships followed an identical pattern. The winners of the one-, two- and three-year-old colt and filly classes competed for the Junior Challenge Cups that had been presented respectively by Lady Wentworth and Lieutenant-Colonel T. R. Badger. These champions then came forward with the winners of the Stallion, Mare and Broodmare classes to contest the Supreme Championships. The best stallion received a Challenge Cup presented by Mrs H. V. Musgrave Clark, and the female winner a medal presented by the Society.

This somewhat discriminatory arrangement continued until 1965 when a Challenge Cup for the best mare or filly was presented by Mrs E. M. Thomas. In the same year she also donated a Challenge Cup for the best stallion or colt. This outranked Mrs Clark's award which had been restricted to stallions only and its winner became the Male Champion of the Show. In 1969, Mrs Bazy Tankersley, owner of the Al-Marah Stud in the United States, gave a cup for the Mare Champion so that there were at this stage six Championships at each Show: Junior Male and Female, Male and Female Champions of the Show, Stallion Champion and Mare Champion.

Thus matters remained until 1985 when the system was simplified and the number of relevant Championships reduced to four – male and female, junior and senior.

The terms Junior Male and Female Champions have been used throughout the period covered by this book. From 1953 through 1984, the Champions of the Show have been called Supreme Male and Supreme Female Champions and, from 1985 to the present, Senior Male and Female Champions. In those years where a Junior Champion also took the Supreme award, an illustration of the appropriate Mare or Stallion Champion has been included.

## Strains

A number of horses have, instead of a strain name, the description 'Veragua Mare' or (for instance) 'Family of Elsissa Or.Ar.'. This calls for an explanation.

During the Spanish Civil War, the Duke of Veragua was killed and all papers relating to his stud destroyed. Some of the mares that survived the war were known but several of the older fillies could not be identified, excepting that they were the Duke's pure Arabians. These fillies were given names beginning with *Vera* and have since been customarily treated as the foundation mares of the *Vera* lines of descent. As all Arabian horses take their strain from their desert-bred foundation mares, it will readily be understood that no strain could be attached to the *Vera* lines. A fuller account may be found in Maxwell, *Spanish Arabian Horse Families*, page 10.

In the case of Elsissa Or.Ar. and others, the lines are in general of such antiquity that the strain name of the founding female has been lost during the passage of time. Readers who wish either to delve more deeply into these matters, or to take the pedigrees back to their foundation animals, may usefully refer to the following handbooks:

Fahlgren, B. *The Arabian Horse Families of Poland 1790-1987* (Heriot)
Gazder, Dr P. *The Arab Horse Families of Great Britain 1875-1973* (Heriot)
Kale, H. Jr. *The Russian Arab Studbook, Volumes 1 through 4* (Kale)
Maxwell, J. *Spanish Arabian Horse Families 1898-1978* (Heriot)
Pearson, C. & Mol, K. *The Arabian Horse Families of Egypt 1870-1980* (Heriot)

## Illustrations

With a few, usually obvious, exceptions, all the photographs in this collection were taken at the Show in the year in which the horses won their Championships. In the case of multiple winners, the best and most representative photograph of the horse has been printed.

*AHSB Volume XVII* is the volume pending in which horses are currently being registered and will cover the years 1990 through 1993.

## Abbreviations

| | |
|---|---|
| AHRA | Arabian Horse Registry of America |
| AHSB | Arab Horse Stud Book of Great Britain |
| AHSB Aust. | Arab Horse Stud Book of Australia |
| AVS | Arab Horse Stud Book of the Netherlands |
| FA | Arab Horse Stud Book of Sweden |
| PASB | Polish Arab Stud Book |
| RASB | Russian Arab Stud Book |
| SBC BA | Arab Stud Book of Belgium |
| SBE | Spanish Stud Book |
| VZAP | Arab Horse Stud Book of Germany |
| i.i.u. | imported in utero |
| (imp.) | imported – here used solely for horses imported into Britain |

## Show Venues

| | | | |
|---|---|---|---|
| 1953 to 1957 | Roehampton | 1975 and 1976 | Peterborough |
| 1958 | Richmond | 1977 to 1988 | Ascot |
| 1959 to 1972 | Kempton Park | 1989 | Kempton Park |
| 1973 and 1974 | Syon Park | 1990 to 1992 | Malvern |

# INDEX OF CHAMPIONS
## ARRANGED CHRONOLOGICALLY

8

9

# LINES OF DESCENT

The following pages are intended as a sketchmap only. They are based solely upon champions' lines of descent in tail male and are restricted to families containing two or more winners. Dates in brackets are dates of birth. Male champions are shown in **BOLD** capitals and female champions in **bold** upper/lower case.

*The Line from MESAOUD imp. 1887*
Mesaoud through:
  RADI (1925)
    **BRIGHT SHADOW** (1948) in 1959
      **Silver Sheen** (1962) in 1963, 1964, 1968, 1969 and 1970

  MANASSEH (1937)
    **DARGEE** (1945) in 1955 and 1960
    **CRYSTAL FIRE** (1952) in 1955
      **Crystal Magic** (1958) in 1961
    **DARJEEL** (1962) in 1965, 1968, 1969 and 1970
      **Bint Ludoet** (1979) in 1986
      RIAZ (1974)
        **Riazana** (1984) in 1986
    **Sirella** (1953) in 1956, 1959 and 1962

  ORAN (1940)
    **GRAND ROYAL** (1947) in 1953 and 1956
    **ROYAL GLITTER** (1954) in 1956
    **Rajjela** (1957) in 1959
    ROYAL DIAMOND (1948)
      **Silver Grey** (1957) in 1960, 1963 and 1965
    **SILVER VANITY** (1950)
      HANIF (1962)
        **Zarafah** (1978) in 1980
      **HAROUN** (1968) in 1971, 1972 and 1974
        MEHRIZ (1973)
          **MEHZEER** (1979) in 1982
        SHAHIR (1973)
          **Shahlie** (1977) in 1984
        **Harida** (1973) in 1989

Mesaoud through Oran (cont.)
 ORAN
  INDIAN KING (1953)
   DANCING KING (1961)
    **RADFAN** (1964) in 1967
    **SUNLIGHT'S ALLEGRO** (1964) in 1966
     **MALACHI** (1972) in 1973
     **Al Shamsa** (1969) in 1979
   CRYSTAL KING (1969)
    **GRAND DUKE** (1974) in 1976
    CRYSTAL MAGICIAN (1977)
     **Tarantara** (1980) in 1983
     **Spey Crystal** (1982) in 1985
   SONG OF INDIA (1986)
    **MYROS** (1972) in 1980
   **Indian Sylphette** (1976) in 1982
  NORAN (1956)
   **ACHIM** imp. (1961) in 1973 and 1983
  **ORION** (1965) in 1971 and 1976
   **Bright Venus** (1973) in 1975 and 1976
  **Silver Shadow** (1946) in 1953
  **Crown of Destiny** (1951) in 1953
  **Silent Wings** (1954) in 1957
  **Nerinora** (1954) in 1958
  **African Queen** (1956) in 1968

*The Line from SKOWRONEK imp. 1913*
Skowronek through:
 NASEEM (1922) exported to the USSR in 1936
  IREX (1927)
   CHAMPURRADO (1940)
    **Sherifa** (1946) in 1957
    **BENJAMIN** (1946) in 1963
     ST. SIMON (1973)
      **Sianah Gold** (1978) in 1987
    **SHAMMAR** (1955) in 1964
     CARBINE (1970)
      MUSKETEER (1974)
       **Zemire** (1977) in 1978
  IRIDOS (1951)
   **KAMI** (1957) in 1960

Skowronek through Naseem (cont.)
  NASEEM
    RAKTHA (1934)
      STAR DIAMOND (1943)
        STARGARD (1951)
          Elara (1962) in 1965
          SHARZAR (1971) in 1975
      INDIAN MAGIC (1944) in 1957
        Yemama (1959) in 1962
        SCINDIAN MAGIC (1961)
          Sheer Magic (1967) in 1974, 1976 and 1977
        INDRISS (1961)
          NASIB (1971) in 1974
        INDIAN FLAME II (1964)
          SILVER FLAME (1970) in 1982
        ASTUR (1966) in 1969
        MAJAL (1966) in 1968
        INDIAN SILVER (1970)
          Aliha (1977) in 1991
      GENERAL GRANT (1945)
        CHIEF KASALO (1950)
        Teresita (1951) in 1954
        Eloia (1952) in 1960
        Amorella (1964) in 1967
        Cydella (1968) in 1970
        Blue Iris (1969) in 1971
        Blue Fashion (1971) in 1973
        GENERAL GOLD (1973) in 1979
    NEGATIW (1945)
      NABOR (1950)
        ARGOS imp. (1957)
          MAGIC ARGOSY (1967)
            Vonitsa (1972) in 1974
        SALON (1959)
          MOMENT (1969)
            NARIM imp. (1980)
              NAYEF (1988) in 1991

Skowronek through Naseem (cont.)
  NASEEM
    NEGATIW (cont.)
      GON (1964)
        PENTAGON (1974)
          **PANDOER "HT"** (1981) in 1990
      NOMER (1943)
        **Napraslina** (1948) in 1967

Skowronek through:
  RASEYN (1923) exported to the USA in 1926
    FERSEYN (1937)
        FERNEYN (1944)
        FERZON (1952)
          GAI WARSAW imp. (1969)
            **IBN WARSAW** (1987) in 1989
          GAI PARADA (1969)
            GAI GASPACHO imp. (1976)
              **Fazleta** (1985) in 1987

*The Line from MAHRUSS II imp. 1897*
Mahruss II through:
  NASIK (1908) exported to the USA in 1926
    RIFNAS (1932)
      AULANI (1940)
        AURAB (1957)
          BEN RABBA imp. (1964)
            AURELIAN (1981)
              **Aureme** (1989) in 1990

  RISSALIX (1934)
    COUNT DORSAZ (1945)
      **COUNT ORLANDO** (1951) in 1954
      **Princess Zia** (1954) in 1955
      COUNT RAPELLO (1954)
        **Ghazali** (1961) in 1972
        **Amaveda** (1966) in 1969
      **SAMSON** (1954) in 1957

Mahruss II through Rissalix (cont.)
  RISSALIX
    COUNT DORSAZ (cont.)
      **Alzehra** (1957) in 1958
      COUNT ROLAND (1957)
        ROXAN (1964)
          THE PRINCE OF ORANGE (1975)
            **Grey Wood Nymph** (1983) in 1990
    BLUE DOMINO (1947)
      LUDO (1953)
        LUDOMINO (1964)
          AHMOUN (1973)
            **SAKER** (1985) in 1988
        LUDREX (1965)
          DONAX (1971)
            **Rishenda** (1976) in 1980
            ZIRCON NAZEER (1984)
              **TAS Fascination** (1991) in 1992
            **Zircon Karisma** (1988) in 1989
        EL SANTO (1968) in 1970
      MANTO (1956) in 1958 and 1959
        **Azara** (1966) in 1973
      BLUE MAGIC (1959) in 1961 and 1962
      GOLDEN DOMINO (1962) in 1963
      FARI II (1965)
        **KING COTTON GOLD** (1971) in 1972
          **MIDNIGHT GOLD** (1976) in 1979
          **BRAVADO** (1976) in 1981
      Sugar Plum Fairy (1958) in 1966
      **Domatella** (1960) in 1971
    MIKENO (1949) in 1961
      EL MELUK (1959) in 1966 and 1967
      RAJMEK (1961) in 1964 and 1965
      SHAHID (1970)
        **Najat** (1976) in 1979 and 1981
      **Mikaela** (1970) in 1972

*The Line from JAMIL EL KEBIR Or.Ar.*

Jamil through:
   FADL (1930) exported to the USA in 1932
     FABAH (1950)
       **THE SHAH** imp. (1966) in 1978
         **SHAHPOOR** (1971) in 1988
         **JAMSHID** (1972) in 1975
         INDIAN TREASURE (1975)
           **Shodina** (1979) in 1983


*The Line from SAKLAWI I Or.Ar.*

Saklawi I Or.Ar. through:
  NAZEER (1934)
    ASWAN (1958) exported to the USSR in 1963
      PALAS (1968)
        **Pilarka** imp. (1975) in 1992
        GONDOLIER (1974)
          PEDANT (1980)
            **PLATOON "HT"** imp. (1987) in 1990
    HADBAN ENZAHI (1952) exported to West Germany in 1955
      MAMELUCK (1969)
        MELCHIOR imp. (1974)
          **DAWEISH** (1978) in 1981
          **MUSTAPHAH** (1978) in 1991
          **ALI AL SAID** (1982) in 1983
      MALIK (1970)
        IBN ESTASHA (1980)
         **ESTA-ESPASHAN** imp. (1983) in 1989
    IBN FAKHRI (1952)
      FAKHR EL KHEIL imp. (1970)
        EL KHERON (1977)
         **Farahnaz** (1981) in 1982
    MORAFIC (1956) exported to the USA in 1965
      SHAKER EL MASRI (1963)
        **EL SHAKLAN** imp. (1975) in 1977 and 1978
          **MALEIK EL KHEIL** (1979) in 1980
            **KURAISHI** (1983) in 1986
        IBN ESTOPA imp. (1977)
         **ESTASAN IBN ESTOPA** imp. (1984) in 1987

Saklawi I Or.Ar. through Nazeer (cont.)
  NAZEER
    TALAL (1957) exported to the USA in 1967
      THE PURITAN (1970)
        RALVON NAZARENE (1974)
          **RALVON ELIJAH** imp. (1978) in 1984 and 1985
    IBN HALIMA (1978) exported to the USA in 1959
      ANSATA HALIM SHAH (1980)
        SALAA EL DINE (1985)
          **CRUSADER** (1990) in 1992


*The Line from KRYZYK Or.Ar.*
Kryzyk Or.Ar. through:
  EL AZRAK (1960)
    **BANAT** imp. (1967) in 1977
      **TRIUMPHAL CHANT** (1976) in 1986


*The Line from SEANDERICH Or.Ar.*
Seanderich Or.Ar. through:
  CONGO (1941)
    TABAL (1952)
      JACIO (1968)
        GHADAMES imp. (1978)
          **ESPLENDOR** (1983) in 1984
          **Kahramana** (1983) in 1984
    ZANCUDO (1958)
      JABALPUR (1968)
        **Hagunia** imp. (1975) in 1985

  SHERIF (1943)
    ALCAZAR (1959)
      **Kadidja** imp. (1969) in 1978

*The Line from LATIF Or.Ar.*

Latif Or.Ar. through:
   KOREJ (1939)
     KNIPPEL (1954)
       **Nahodka** imp. (1963) in 1975
    MAK (1956)
      KUMIR (1973)
        PAKISTAN (1979)
          **BESPECHNI** imp. (1987) in 1992

# Chief Kasalo

Junior Male Champion 1953

| | | | |
|---|---|---|---|
| | | | Naseem |
| | | Raktha | |
| | | | Razina |
| | General Grant | | |
| | | | Riffal |
| CHIEF KASALO | | Samsie | |
| Chestnut Colt – 1950 | | | Naxina |
| Kehailan Rodan | | | Faris |
| AHSB Volume VIII | | Rissalix | |
| | | | Rissla |
| | Rikitea | | |
| | | | Nuri Sherif |
| | | Nurschida | |
| | | | Razina |

Bred and exhibited by Miss G. Yule     Exported to South Africa in 1954

# Crown of Destiny

Junior Female Champion 1953

| | | | |
|---|---|---|---|
| | | Riffal | Naufal |
| | | | Razina |
| | Oran | | |
| CROWN OF DESTINY | | Astrella | Raseem |
| Chestnut Filly – 1951 | | | Amida |
| Kehaileh Dajanieh | | | Naseem |
| AHSB Volume VIII | | Raktha | |
| | | | Razina |
| | Grey Royal | | |
| | | Sharima | Shareer |
| | | | Nashisha |

Bred and exhibited by Lady Wentworth          Exported to the USA in 1957

# Grand Royal

*Photonews*

## Supreme Male Champion 1953 and 1956

|  |  |  |  |
|---|---|---|---|
|  |  | Riffal | Naufal |
|  | Oran |  | Razina |
| GRAND ROYAL |  | Astrella | Raseem |
| Chestnut Stallion – 1947 |  |  | Amida |
| Kehailan Dajani |  | Shareer | Nureddin II |
| AHSB Volume VII |  |  | Selima |
|  | Sharima |  | Rasim |
|  |  | Nashisha | Nasra |

Bred and exhibited by Lady Wentworth          Exported to Australia in 1959

# Silver Shadow

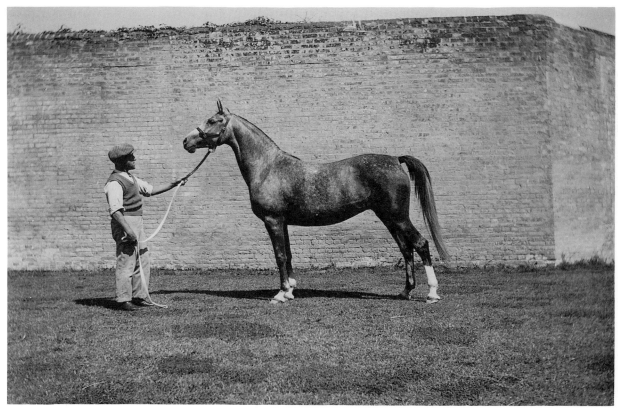

Photo: Mrs R. Archer

## Supreme Female Champion 1953

|  |  | Riffal | Naufal |
|---|---|---|---|
|  | Oran |  | Razina |
| SILVER SHADOW |  | Astrella | Raseem |
| Grey Mare – 1946 |  |  | Amida |
| Hamdanieh Simrieh |  | Naseem | Skowronek (imp.) |
| AHSB Volume VII |  |  | Nasra |
|  | Silver Fire |  | Daoud |
|  |  | Somra | Siwa |

Bred and exhibited by Lady Wentworth

# Count Orlando

*Photonews*

## Junior Male Champion 1954

|  |  |  | Faris |
|---|---|---|---|
|  |  | Rissalix | Rissla |
|  | Count Dorsaz |  | Naziri |
|  |  | Shamnar | Razina |
| COUNT ORLANDO |  |  | Riffal |
| Chestnut Colt – 1951 |  | Oran | Astrella |
| Kehailan Ajuz |  |  | Algol |
| AHSB Volume VIII | Umatella |  | Nurschida |
|  |  | Namilla |  |

Bred and exhibited by Miss G. Yule          Exported to the USA in 1960

23

# *Teresita*

*Photonews*

Junior and Supreme Female Champion 1954

| | | | |
|---|---|---|---|
| | | Raktha | Naseem |
| | General Grant | | Razina |
| | | Samsie | Riffal |
| TERESITA | | | Naxina |
| Chestnut Filly – 1951 | | | |
| Kehaileh Rodanieh | | Rissalix | Faris |
| AHSB Volume VIII | | | Rissla |
| | Rikitea | | |
| | | Nurschida | Nuri Sherif |
| | | | Razina |

Exhibited by Miss M. Greely
Bred by Miss G. Yule

# Bahram

*Photonews*

Supreme Male Champion 1954

|  |  |  | Feysul (imp.) |
|---|---|---|---|
|  |  | Rasim | |
|  |  | | Risala |
|  | Sainfoin | | |
|  | | | Berk |
| | | Safarjal | |
| BAHRAM | | | Somra |
| Chestnut Stallion – 1946 | | | |
| Seglawi Jedran | | | |
| AHSB Volume VII | | Fedaan Or.Ar. (imp.) | |
| | Betina | | |
| | | | Rijm |
| | | Belka | |
| | | | Bereyda |

Bred and exhibited by Mr H. V. Musgrave Clark

# Crystal Fire

*Photonews*

Junior Male Champion 1955

|  |  |  | Joseph |
|---|---|---|---|
|  |  | Manasseh | Aatika |
|  | Dargee |  | Algol |
| CRYSTAL FIRE |  | Myola | Rythma |
| Chestnut Colt – 1952 |  |  | Riffal |
| Kehailan Rodan |  | Oran | Astrella |
| AHSB Volume VIII | Rosinella |  | Indian Gold |
|  |  | Rosalina | Rissella |

Bred and exhibited by Mrs S. Bomford        Exported to Australia in 1961

# *Princess Zia*

Photonews

Junior and Supreme Female Champion 1955

| | | | |
|---|---|---|---|
| | | Rissalix | Faris |
| | | | Rissla |
| | Count Dorsaz | | |
| | | Shamnar | Naziri |
| PRINCESS ZIA | | | Razina |
| Chestnut Filly – 1954 | | | |
| Kehaileh Rodanieh | | Radi | Rishan |
| AHSB Volume VIII | | | Razina |
| | Queen Zenobia | | |
| | | Sulka | Naseem |
| | | | Nurschida |

Bred and exhibited by Miss G. Yule          Exported to the USA in 1966

27

# Dargee

*Photonews*

## Supreme Male Champion 1955 and 1960

|  |  |  | Nadir |
|---|---|---|---|
|  |  | Joseph | Maisuna |
|  | Manasseh |  | Algol |
| DARGEE |  | Aatika | Rizada |
| Chestnut Stallion – 1945 |  |  | Aldebaran |
| Kehailan Rodan |  | Algol | Rangha |
| AHSB Volume VII | Myola |  | Berk |
|  |  | Rythma | Risala |

Exhibited by Lady Wentworth
Bred by Mr G. H. Ruxton

# Royal Glitter

*Photonews*

## Junior Male Champion 1956

| | | | |
|---|---|---|---|
| ROYAL GLITTER Bay Colt – 1954 Kehailan Dajani AHSB Volume VIII | Grand Royal | Oran | Riffal |
| | | | Astrella |
| | | Sharima | Shareer |
| | | | Nashisha |
| | Silver Gilt | Indian Gold | Ferhan |
| | | | Nisreen |
| | | Silver Fire | Naseem |
| | | | Somra |

Bred and exhibited by Lady Wentworth

# Sirella

Junior and Supreme Female Champion 1956
Supreme Female Champion 1959 and 1962

|  |  |  | Joseph |
|  |  | Manasseh | |
|  |  | | Aatika |
|  | Dargee | | |
|  | | | Algol |
| SIRELLA | | Myola | |
| Chestnut Mare – 1953 | | | Rythma |
| Kehaileh Dajanieh | | | Naseem |
| AHSB Volume VIII | | Rissam | |
|  | | | Rim |
|  | Shalina | | |
|  | | | Rytham |
|  | | Sharfina | |
|  | | | Sharima |

Exhibited by Lady Wentworth in 1956 and Mr C. G. Covey in 1959 and 1962
Bred by Lady Wentworth

Sirella in 1956                    *Photonews*

Sirella in 1962                    *Photonews*

# Samson

*Photonews*

Junior Male Champion 1957

| | | | |
|---|---|---|---|
| | | Rissalix | Faris |
| | Count Dorsaz | | Rissla |
| | | Shamnar | Naziri |
| SAMSON | | | Razina |
| Bay Colt – 1954 | | | Naufal |
| Kehailan Dajani | | Riffal | Razina |
| AHSB Volume VIII | Samsie | | Skowronek (imp.) |
| | | Naxina | Nessima |

Bred and exhibited by Miss G. Yule

# Silent Wings

*Photonews*

Junior Female Champion 1957

| | | |
|---|---|---|
| | | Naufal |
| | Riffal | Razina |
| Oran | | Raseem |
| SILENT WINGS | Astrella | Amida |
| Chestnut Filly – 1954 | | Ferhan |
| Kehaileh Dajanieh | Indian Gold | Nisreen |
| AHSB Volume VIII | | |
| Silfina | | Rytham |
| | Sharfina | Sharima |

**SILENT WINGS**
Chestnut Filly – 1954
Kehaileh Dajanieh
AHSB Volume VIII

Bred and exhibited by Lady Wentworth

33

# Indian Magic

*Photonews*

Supreme Male Champion 1957

| | | | |
|---|---|---|---|
| | | Naseem | Skowronek (imp.) |
| | | | Nasra |
| | Raktha | | Rasim |
| INDIAN MAGIC | | Razina | Riyala |
| Grey Stallion – 1944 | | | Rasim |
| Kehailan Dajani | | Raseem | |
| AHSB Volume VII | | | Rim |
| | Indian Crown | | Nureddin II |
| | | Nisreen | Nasra |

Bred and exhibited by Lady Wentworth

34

# Sherifa

*Photonews*

## Supreme Female Champion 1957

|  |  |  | Naseem |
|---|---|---|---|
|  |  | Irex | |
|  | Champurrado | | Rissla |
|  |  |  | Rissam |
| SHERIFA |  | Niseyra | |
| Chestnut Mare – 1946 |  |  | Neraida |
| Hamdanieh Simrieh |  |  | |
| AHSB Volume VII |  | Fedaan Or.Ar. (imp.) | |
|  | Somra II | | |
|  |  |  | Berk |
|  |  | Safarjal | |
|  |  |  | Somra |

Bred and exhibited by Mr H. V. Musgrave Clark

Photo: C. Mass

# *Manto*

Junior Male Champion 1958 and 1959

| | | | |
|---|---|---|---|
| | | Rissalix | Faris |
| | Blue Domino | | Rissla |
| MANTO | | Niseyra | Rissam |
| Liver Chestnut Colt – 1956 | | | Neraida |
| Kehailan Rodan | | Oran | Riffal |
| AHSB Volume VIII | | | Astrella |
| | Mifaria | Rithyana | Raktha |
| | | | Rishyana |

Bred and exhibited by Lady Anne Lytton

# Alzehra

*Photonews*

Junior Female Champion 1958

| | | | |
|---|---|---|---|
| | | Rissalix | Faris |
| | | | Rissla |
| | Count Dorsaz | | Naziri |
| ALZEHRA | | Shamnar | Razina |
| Chestnut Filly – 1957 | | | Naseem |
| Wadna Khirsanieh | | Irex | Rissla |
| AHSB Volume IX | Zehraa | | Manak Or.Ar.(imp.) |
| | | Nurmana | Nuhra Or.Ar. (imp.) |

Bred and exhibited by Lady May Abel Smith

37

*Photone*

# *Silver Vanity*

## Supreme Male Champion 1958 and 1962

| | | | Naufal |
|---|---|---|---|
| | | Riffal | |
| | | | Razina |
| | Oran | | |
| | | | Raseem |
| SILVER VANITY | | Astrella | |
| Grey Stallion – 1950 | | | Amida |
| Hamdani Simri | | | |
| AHSB Volume VIII | | | Ferhan |
| | | Indian Gold | |
| | | | Nisreen |
| | Silver Gilt | | |
| | | | Naseem |
| | | Silver Fire | |
| | | | Somra |

Exhibited by Mr C. G. Covey          Exported to the USA in 1962
Bred by Lady Wentworth

# Nerinora

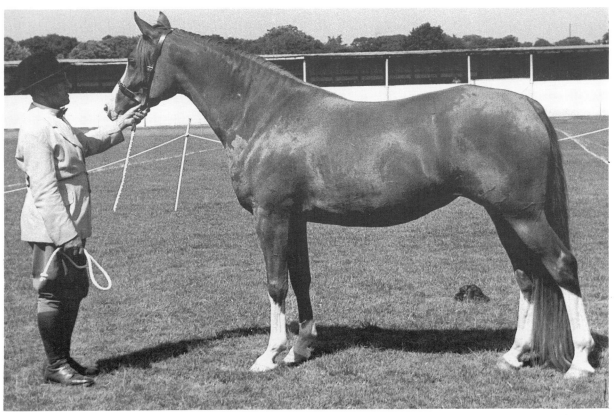

*Photonews*

Supreme Female Champion 1958

| | | | |
|---|---|---|---|
| NERINORA<br>Chestnut Mare – 1954<br>Kehaileh Rodanieh<br>AHSB Volume IX | Oran | Riffal | Naufal |
| | | | Razina |
| | | Astrella | Raseem |
| | | | Amida |
| | Nerina | Rissalix | Faris |
| | | | Rissla |
| | | Risira | Naziri |
| | | | Risslina |

Exhibited by Mr C. G. Covey
Bred by Lady Wentworth

# Rajjela

*Photonews*

Junior Female Champion 1959

|  |  |  |  |
|---|---|---|---|
|  |  | Oran | Riffal |
|  | Grand Royal |  | Astrella |
| RAJJELA |  | Sharima | Shareer |
| Chestnut Filly – 1957 |  |  | Nashisha |
| Wadna Khirsanieh |  | Irex | Naseem |
| AHSB Volume IX | Nuhajjela |  | Rissla |
|  |  | Nuhra Or.Ar. (imp.) |  |

Bred and exhibited by Lady May Abel Smith

# Bright Shadow

*Photonews*

Supreme Male Champion 1959

| | | |
|---|---|---|
| | | Nadir |
| | Rishan | Rish |
| Radi | | Rasim |
| | Razina | Riyala |
| | | Faris |
| | Rissalix | Rissla |
| Pale Shadow | | Naziri |
| | Shamnar | Razina |

BRIGHT SHADOW
Chestnut Stallion – 1948
Kehailan Rodan
AHSB Volume VII

Exhibited by Mr C. G. Covey
Bred by Lady Wentworth

41

# *Kami*

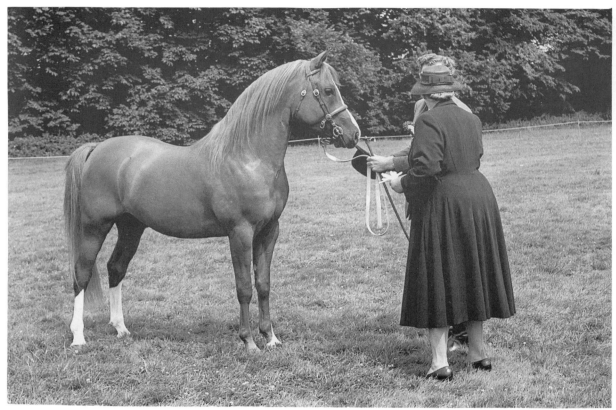

*Photonews*

Junior Male Champion 1960

|  |  | Irex | Naseem |
|  |  |  | Rissla |
|  | Iridos |  |  |
| KAMI |  | Rafeena | Aluf |
| Chestnut Colt – 1957 |  |  | Ranya II |
| Kehailan Rodan |  |  | Faris |
| AHSB Volume IX |  | Rissalix | Rissla |
|  | Kabara |  |  |
|  |  | Shamnar | Naziri |
|  |  |  | Razina |

Bred and exhibited by Miss M. Evans

# Silver Grey

*Photonews*

Junior Female Champion 1960
Supreme Female Champion 1963 and 1965

| | | | |
|---|---|---|---|
| SILVER GREY<br>Grey Mare – 1957<br>Hamdanieh Simrieh<br>AHSB Volume IX | Royal Diamond | Oran | Riffal |
| | | | Astrella |
| | | Grey Royal | Raktha |
| | | | Sharima |
| | Silver Gilt | Indian Gold | Ferhan |
| | | | Nisreen |
| | | Silver Fire | Naseem |
| | | | Somra |

Exhibited by Mr C. G. Covey
Bred by Lady Wentworth

# *Eloia*

## Supreme Female Champion 1960

|  |  |  |  |
|---|---|---|---|
|  |  |  | Naseem |
|  |  | Raktha |  |
|  |  |  | Razina |
|  | General Grant |  |  |
|  |  |  | Riffal |
| ELOIA |  | Samsie |  |
| Chestnut Mare – 1952 |  |  | Naxina |
| Kehaileh Rodanieh |  |  | Faris |
| AHSB Volume VIII |  | Rissalix |  |
|  |  |  | Rissla |
|  | Elvira |  |  |
|  |  |  | Shihab |
|  |  | Hama |  |
|  |  |  | Razina |

Exhibited by Miss M. Evans
Bred by Miss G. Yule

# Blue Magic

*Photonews*

Junior Male Champion 1961 and 1962

BLUE MAGIC
Chestnut Colt – 1959
Kehailan Dajani
AHSB Volume IX

| | | | |
|---|---|---|---|
| | Blue Domino | Rissalix | Faris |
| | | | Rissla |
| | | Niseyra | Rissam |
| | | | Neraida |
| | Indian Starlight | Indian Magic | Raktha |
| | | | Indian Crown |
| | | Indian Pride | Irex |
| | | | Nisreen |

Exhibited by Mr L. Theobald
Bred by Mr & Mrs D. D. Wright

# Crystal Magic

Junior Female Champion 1961

|                      | Crystal Fire    | Dargee    | Manasseh |
|                      |                 |           | Myola    |
|                      |                 | Rosinella | Oran     |
| CRYSTAL MAGIC        |                 |           | Rosalina |
| Chestnut Filly – 1958 |                 |           | Riffal   |
| Kehaileh Dajanieh    | Royal Exchange  | Oran      | Astrella |
| AHSB Volume IX       |                 | Sharfina  | Rithan   |
|                      |                 |           | Sharima  |

Bred and exhibited by Mrs S. Bomford

46

# *Mikeno*

## Supreme Male Champion 1961

|  |  |  |
|---|---|---|
|  |  | Nureddin II |
|  | Faris |  |
| Rissalix |  | Fejr |
|  |  | Berk |
| MIKENO | Rissla |  |
| Chestnut Stallion  –  1949 |  | Risala |
| Kehailan Rodan |  | Aldebaran |
| AHSB Volume VII | Algol |  |
|  |  | Rangha |
| Namilla |  | Nuri Sherif |
|  | Nurschida |  |
|  |  | Razina |

Exhibited by Mrs H. Linney
Bred by Miss G. Yule

# Celina
*(imp.)*

*Photonews*

## Supreme Female Champion 1961

| | | |
|---|---|---|
| | | Kuhailan Haifi Or.Ar. |
| | Ofir | |
| | | Dziwa |
| Witraz | | |
| | | Fetysz |
| | Makata | |
| | | Gazella II |

CELINA (imp.)
Bay Mare – 1949
Seglawieh (family of Woloszka)
PASB, AHSB Volume IX

| | | |
|---|---|---|
| | | Rasim III |
| | Rasim Pierwszy | |
| | | Fasila |
| Elza | | |
| | | Rasim III |
| | El-Zabibe | |
| | | Karima |

Exhibited by Mr H. V. Musgrave Clark
Bred by Albigowa State Stud, Poland

Imported from Poland in 1958

48

# Yemama

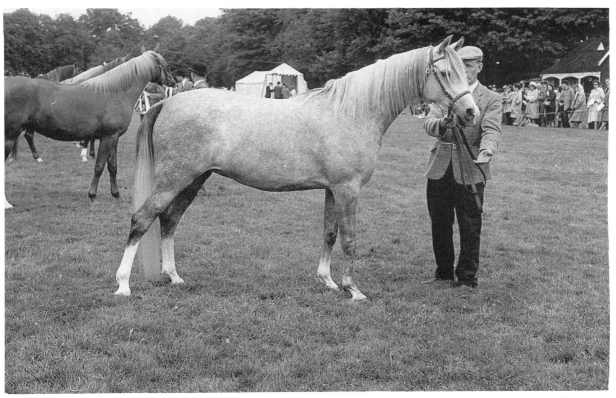

## Junior Female Champion 1962

| | | | |
|---|---|---|---|
| | | Raktha | Naseem |
| | | | Razina |
| | Indian Magic | | Raseem |
| | | Indian Crown | Nisreen |
| YEMAMA | | | Riffal |
| Grey Filly – 1959 | | Oran | |
| Kehaileh Dajanieh | | | Astrella |
| AHSB Volume IX | Silent Wings | | Indian Gold |
| | | Silfina | Sharfina |

Exhibited by Mr & Mrs D. D. Wright
Bred by Mr C. G. Covey

# Golden Domino

*Photonews*

Junior Male Champion 1963

| | | | |
|---|---|---|---|
| | | Rissalix | Faris |
| | Blue Domino | | Rissla |
| GOLDEN DOMINO | | Niseyra | Rissam |
| Chestnut Colt – 1962 | | | Neraida |
| Kehailan Rodan | | Rifari | Faris |
| AHSB Volume IX | | | Risslina |
| | Crystal Dew | | Indian Gold |
| | | Gleaming Gold | Risira |

Bred and exhibited by Mrs I. Scott          Exported to the USA in 1963

# Benjamin

*Photonews*

Supreme Male Champion 1963

| | | Naseem |
|---|---|---|
| | Irex | Rissla |
| Champurrado | | Rissam |
| | Niseyra | Neraida |
| | | Rasim |
| | Sainfoin | Safarjal |
| Baranova | | Nimr Or.Ar. (imp.) |
| | Bekr | Belka |

BENJAMIN
Bay Stallion – 1946
Seglawi Jedran
AHSB Volume VII

Bred and exhibited by Mr H. V. Musgrave Clark

# Silver Sheen

Junior Female Champion 1963 and 1964
Supreme Female Champion 1964, 1968, 1969 and 1970

|  |  |  | Rishan |
| --- | --- | --- | --- |
|  |  | Radi | |
|  |  | | Razina |
|  | Bright Shadow | | |
|  | | | Rissalix |
| SILVER SHEEN | | Pale Shadow | |
| Grey Mare – 1962 | | | Shamnar |
| Hamdanieh Simrieh | | | Oran |
| AHSB Volume XI | | Royal Diamond | |
|  | | | Grey Royal |
|  | Silver Grey | | |
|  | | | Indian Gold |
|  | | Silver Gilt | |
|  | | | Silver Fire |

Exhibited by Mrs E. M. Thomas
Bred by Mr C. G. Covey

Silver Sheen in 1963

Silver Sheen in 1969 with, at foot, Silver Blue by Azrak

# *Rajmek*

*Photonews*

Junior Male Champion 1964
Supreme Male Champion 1965

|  |  |  | Faris |
|  |  | Rissalix |  |
|  | Mikeno |  | Rissla |
|  |  |  | Algol |
| RAJMEK |  | Namilla |  |
| Chestnut Stallion – 1961 |  |  | Nurschida |
| Wadnan Khirsan |  |  | Oran |
| AHSB Volume IX |  | Grand Royal |  |
|  |  |  | Sharima |
|  | Rajjela |  |  |
|  |  |  | Irex |
|  |  | Nuhajjela |  |
|  |  |  | Nuhra Or.Ar. (imp.) |

Bred and exhibited by Lady May Abel Smith

54

# Shammar

*Photonews*

Supreme Male Champion 1964

|  |  |  | Naseem |
|---|---|---|---|
|  |  | Irex | Rissla |
|  | Champurrado |  | Rissam |
| SHAMMAR |  | Niseyra | Neraida |
| Grey Stallion – 1955 |  |  |  |
| Hamdani Simri |  | Fedaan Or.Ar. (imp.) |  |
| AHSB Volume VIII |  |  |  |
|  | Somra II |  | Berk |
|  |  | Safarjal | Somra |

Bred and exhibited by Mr H. V. Musgrave Clark

55

# Darjeel

*Photonews*

Junior Male Champion 1965
Supreme Male Champion 1968, 1969 and 1970

|  |  |  |  |
|---|---|---|---|
|  |  | Manasseh | Joseph |
|  | Dargee |  | Aatika |
| DARJEEL |  | Myola | Algol |
| Chestnut Stallion – 1962 |  |  | Rythma |
| Wadnan Khirsan |  | Grand Royal | Oran |
| AHSB Volume X |  |  | Sharima |
|  | Rajjela |  | Irex |
|  |  | Nuhajjela | Nuhra Or.Ar. (imp.) |

Bred and exhibited by Lady May Abel Smith

56

# *Elara*

## Junior Female Champion 1965

| | | |
|---|---|---|
| **ELARA**<br>Chestnut Filly – 1962<br>Kehaileh Rodanieh<br>AHSB Volume IX | Stargard | Star Diamond |
| | | |
| | | Somara |
| | Eloia | General Grant |
| | | Elvira |

| | | |
|---|---|---|
| Star Diamond | Raktha |
| | Sharima |
| Somara | Nureddin II |
| | Silver Fire |
| General Grant | Raktha |
| | Samsie |
| Elvira | Rissalix |
| | Hama |

Bred and exhibited by Miss M. Evans     Exported to Australia in 1974

# *Sunlight's Allegro*

*Photonews*

Junior Male Champion 1966

|  |  |  | Riffal |
|---|---|---|---|
|  |  | Oran | |
|  |  |  | Astrella |
|  | Indian King | | |
|  |  |  | Irex |
| SUNLIGHT'S ALLEGRO |  | Indian Pride | |
| Chestnut Colt – 1964 |  |  | Nisreen |
| Kehailan Dajani |  |  | Manasseh |
| AHSB Volume X |  | Dargee | |
|  |  |  | Myola |
|  | Dancing Sunlight | | |
|  |  |  | Rissam |
|  |  | Shades of Night | |
|  |  |  | Sharfina |

Bred and exhibited by Mr & Mrs R. M. Kydd

# Lyvia

*Photonews*

Junior Female Champion 1966

| | | |
|---|---|---|
| | | Priboj |
| | Pomeranets | |
| | | Mammona |
| Naplyv (imp.) | | |
| | | Naseem |
| LYVIA | Nitochka | |
| Grey Filly – 1964 | | Taraszcza |
| Kehaileh Dajanieh | | |
| AHSB Volume X | | Riffal |
| | Oran | |
| | | Astrella |
| Extra Special | | |
| | | Rithan |
| | Sharfina | |
| | | Sharima |

Bred and exhibited by Mrs E. M. Thomas

# El Meluk

*Photonews*

Supreme Male Champion 1966 and 1967

| | | | | Faris |
| | | Rissalix | |
| | Mikeno | | | Rissla |
| | | | | Algol |
| EL MELUK | | Namilla | | |
| Chestnut Stallion – 1959 | | | | Nurschida |
| Kehailan Rodan | | | | Riffal |
| AHSB Volume X | | Oran | | |
| | Mifaria | | | Astrella |
| | | | | Raktha |
| | | Rithyana | |
| | | | | Rishyana |

Exhibited by Mrs H. Linney
Bred by Lady Anne Lytton

# Sugar Plum Fairy

*Photonews*

Supreme Female Champion 1966

| | | | |
|---|---|---|---|
| | | Rissalix | Faris |
| | | | Rissla |
| | Blue Domino | | Rissam |
| SUGAR PLUM FAIRY | | Niseyra | Neraida |
| Chestnut Mare – 1958 | | | Aldebaran |
| Kehaileh Rodanieh | | Algol | Rangha |
| AHSB Volume IX | | | |
| | Algoletta | | Berk |
| | | Rythma | Risala |

Exhibited by Mrs E. M. Thomas  
Bred by Mrs S. Bomford

Exported to Israel in 1968

# *Radfan*

Junior Male Champion 1967

|  |  |  | Oran |
|---|---|---|---|
|  |  | Indian King | |
|  | Dancing King | | Indian Pride |
|  |  | | Dargee |
| RADFAN | | Dancing Sunlight | |
| Chestnut Colt – 1964 | | | Shades of Night |
| Kehailan Ajuz | | | Rissalix |
| AHSB Volume X | | Blue Domino | |
|  | | | Niseyra |
|  | Bint Yasimet | | |
|  | | | Grey Owl |
|  | | Yasimet | |
|  | | | Bint Yasim |

Exhibited by Miss E. K. Jones
Bred by Mr & Mrs D. D. Wright

# *Amorella*

*Photonews*

Junior Female Champion 1967

| | | | Naseem |
|---|---|---|---|
| | | Raktha | |
| | General Grant | | Razina |
| | | | Riffal |
| AMORELLA | | Samsie | |
| Chestnut Filly – 1964 | | | Naxina |
| Kehaileh Rodanieh | | | Rissalix |
| AHSB Volume X | | Blue Domino | |
| | Domatella | | Niseyra |
| | | | Oran |
| | | Umatella | |
| | | | Namilla |

Bred and exhibited by Major & Mrs T. W. I. Hedley

63

# Napraslina
## (imp.)

*Photonews*

## Supreme Female Champion 1967

| | | | |
|---|---|---|---|
| | | Naseem | Skowronek (imp.) |
| | | | Nasra |
| | Nomer | | |
| NAPRASLINA (imp.) | | Oaza | Kuhailan Haifi Or.Ar. |
| Grey Mare – 1948 | | | Kewa |
| Family of Elsissa Or.Ar. | | | |
| RASB, AHSB Volume X | | Koheilan I | Koheilan IV |
| | | | 10 Gazal |
| | Plotka | | |
| | | Gaweda | Burgas Or.Ar. |
| | | | Bialogrodka |

Exhibited by Miss M. Evans          Imported from the USSR in 1965
Bred by Tersk Stud, USSR

# *Majal*

*Photonews*

Junior Male Champion 1968

| | | | |
|---|---|---|---|
| | | Raktha | Naseem |
| | Indian Magic | | Razina |
| | | Indian Crown | Raseem |
| MAJAL | | | Nisreen |
| Chestnut Colt – 1966 | | Oran | Riffal |
| Kehailan Rodan | | | Astrella |
| AHSB Volume XI | Mifaria | Rithyana | Raktha |
| | | | Rishyana |

Bred and exhibited by Lady Anne Lytton

# African Queen

*Photonews*

## Junior Female Champion 1968

|  |  | Riffal | Naufal |
|  |  |  | Razina |
|  | Oran |  |  |
|  |  | Astrella | Raseem |
| AFRICAN QUEEN |  |  | Amida |
| Chestnut Filly – 1965 |  |  |  |
| Kehaileh Dajanieh |  | Dargee | Manasseh |
| AHSB Volume X |  |  | Myola |
|  | Incoronetta |  |  |
|  |  | Indian Crown | Raseem |
|  |  |  | Nisreen |

Bred and exhibited by Mrs E. M. Thomas

# Astur

Junior Male Champion 1969

| | | | |
|---|---|---|---|
| | | Raktha | Naseem |
| | Indian Magic | | Razina |
| | | Indian Crown | Raseem |
| ASTUR | | | Nisreen |
| Grey Stallion – 1966 | | | |
| Kehailan Rodan | | Dargee | Manasseh |
| AHSB Volume XI | Rissalma | | Myola |
| | | Rissiletta | Indian Gold |
| | | | Rissla |

Bred and exhibited by Mrs E. M. Thomas

# Amaveda

## Junior Female Champion 1969

| | | | |
|---|---|---|---|
| | | Count Dorsaz | Rissalix |
| | Count Rapello | | Shamnar |
| AMAVEDA | | Rafeena | Aluf |
| Chestnut Filly – 1966 | | | Ranya II |
| Kehaileh Dajanieh | | Blue Domino | Rissalix |
| AHSB Volume XI | Samaveda | | Niseyra |
| | | Samsie | Riffal |
| | | | Naxina |

Bred and exhibited by Major & Mrs T. W. I. Hedley

# *El Santo*

Junior Male Champion 1970

| | | | |
|---|---|---|---|
| | | | Rissalix |
| | | Blue Domino | |
| | Ludo | | Niseyra |
| | | | Raktha |
| EL SANTO | | Rithyana | |
| Chestnut Colt – 1968 | | | Rishyana |
| Kehailan Dajani | | | Rissam |
| AHSB Volume XI | | Nizzam | |
| | Nishida (imp.) | | Nezma |
| | | | General Grant |
| | | Bashida | |
| | | | Tehoura |

Bred and exhibited by Mr & Mrs D. D. Wright

69

# Cydella

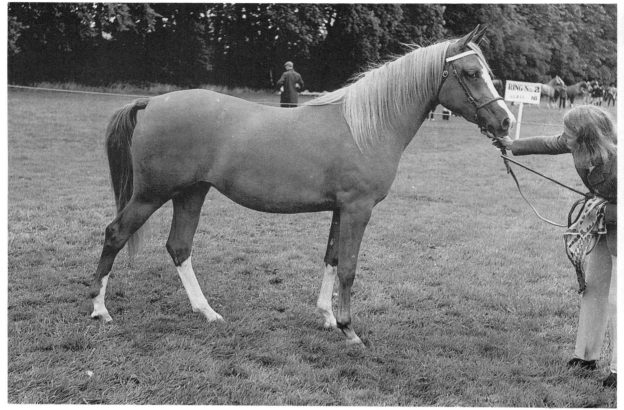

*Photonews*

Junior Female Champion 1970

|  |  | Raktha | Naseem |
|  |  |  | Razina |
|  | General Grant |  |  |
| CYDELLA |  | Samsie | Riffal |
| Chestnut Filly – 1968 |  |  | Naxina |
| Kehaileh Rodanieh |  | Blue Domino | Rissalix |
| AHSB Volume XI |  |  | Niseyra |
|  | Domatella |  |  |
|  |  | Umatella | Oran |
|  |  |  | Namilla |

Bred and exhibited by Major & Mrs T. W. I. Hedley

Photo: Peter Sweet

# Haroun

Junior Male Champion 1971
Stallion Champion 1972
Supreme Male Champion 1974

|  |  |  |
|---|---|---|
|  |  | Oran |
|  | Silver Vanity |  |
|  |  | Silver Gilt |
| Hanif |  |  |
|  |  | Dargee |
| HAROUN | Sirella |  |
| Grey Stallion – 1968 |  | Shalina |
| Kehailan Dajani |  | Blue Domino |
| AHSB Volume XI | Ludo |  |
|  |  | Rithyana |
| Indian Snowflake |  |  |
|  |  | Indian Magic |
|  | Indian Starlight |  |
|  |  | Indian Pride |

Bred and exhibited by Mr M. A. Pitt-Rivers          Exported to Qatar in 1982

# *Blue Iris*

*Photonews*

Junior Female Champion 1971

| | | | |
|---|---|---|---|
| | | Raktha | Naseem |
| | General Grant | | Razina |
| | | | Riffal |
| BLUE IRIS | | Samsie | Naxina |
| Chestnut Filly – 1969 | | | Rissalix |
| Kehaileh Rodanieh | | Blue Domino | Niseyra |
| AHSB Volume XI | Blue Rhapsody | | Joseph |
| | | Roxelana | Roxana |

Bred and exhibited by Major & Mrs T. W. I. Hedley

# Orion

Photo: Ellen Egberts

## Supreme Male Champion 1971 and 1976

|  |  | Riffal | Naufal |
|---|---|---|---|
|  | Oran |  | Razina |
|  |  | Astrella | Raseem |
| ORION |  |  | Amida |
| Chestnut Stallion – 1965 |  | Royal Diamond | Oran |
| Kehailan Dajani |  |  | Grey Royal |
| AHSB Volume X | Dancing Diamond |  | Indian Gold |
|  |  | Dancing Star | Shades of Night |

Exhibited by Major & Mrs T. W. I. Hedley
Bred by Mr C. G. Covey

# Domatella

## Supreme Female Champion 1971

|  |  |  | Faris |
|---|---|---|---|
|  |  | Rissalix | |
|  | Blue Domino | | Rissla |
| DOMATELLA | | | Rissam |
| Chestnut Mare – 1960 | | Niseyra | |
| Kehaileh Rodanieh | | | Neraida |
| AHSB Volume IX | | | Riffal |
| . | | Oran | |
|  | Umatella | | Astrella |
|  | | | Algol |
|  | | Namilla | |
|  | | | Nurschida |

Bred and exhibited by Major & Mrs T. W. I. Hedley

# King Cotton Gold

*Photonews*

Junior and Supreme Male Champion 1972

| | | | |
|---|---|---|---|
| | | Blue Domino | Rissalix |
| | Fari II | | Niseyra |
| | | | Rifari |
| KING COTTON GOLD | | Farette | Shabrette |
| Bay Stallion – 1971 | | | Rissalix |
| Kehailan Rodan | | Blue Domino | Niseyra |
| AHSB Volume XII | Dreaming Gold | | Indian Gold |
| | | Gleaming Gold | Risira |

Bred and exhibited by Mrs P. A. M. Murray

75

# Mikaela

*Photonews*

Junior Female Champion 1972

| | | | |
|---|---|---|---|
| | | Rissalix | Faris |
| | Mikeno | | Rissla |
| MIKAELA | | Namilla | Algol |
| Chestnut Filly – 1970 | | | Nurschida |
| Kehaileh Rodanieh | | General Grant | Raktha |
| AHSB Volume XII | | | Samsie |
| | Chantarella | | Blue Domino |
| | | Domatella | Umatella |

Bred and exhibited by Major & Mrs T. W. I. Hedley

# Ghazali

*Photonews*

Supreme Female Champion 1972

| | | | |
|---|---|---|---|
| | | Count Dorsaz | Rissalix |
| | Count Rapello | | Shamnar |
| GHAZALI | | Rafeena | Aluf |
| Chestnut Mare – 1961 | | | Ranya II |
| Kehaileh Rodanieh | | Raktha | Naseem |
| AHSB Volume IX | Rithyana | | Razina |
| | | Rishyana | Rissam |
| | | | Rishna |

Bred and exhibited by Major & Mrs T. W. I. Hedley

# Malachi

Junior Male Champion 1973

|  |  |  | Oran |
|---|---|---|---|
|  |  | Indian King | Indian Pride |
|  | Sunlight's Allegro |  |  |
| MALACHI |  | Dancing Sunlight | Dargee |
| Chestnut Colt – 1972 |  |  | Shades of Night |
| Kehailan Rodan |  |  | Raktha |
| AHSB Volume XII |  | General Grant | Indian Crown |
|  | Ranee |  |  |
|  |  | Rexeena | Irex |
|  |  |  | Rafeena |

Bred and exhibited by
The Countess of Pembroke

Exported to the Netherlands in 1976

# *Blue Fashion*

*Photo: Deidre Hyde*

Junior Female Champion 1973

| | | | |
|---|---|---|---|
| BLUE FASHION<br>Chestnut Filly – 1971<br>Kehaileh Rodanieh<br>AHSB Volume XII | General Grant | Raktha | Naseem |
| | | | Razina |
| | | Samsie | Riffal |
| | | | Naxina |
| | Blue Rhapsody | Blue Domino | Rissalix |
| | | | Niseyra |
| | | Roxelana | Joseph |
| | | | Roxana |

Bred and exhibited by Major & Mrs T. W. I. Hedley

79

*Photonew*

# *Achim*
## *(imp.)*

### Supreme Male Champion 1973
### Stallion Champion 1983

| | | | |
|---|---|---|---|
| | | | Riffal |
| | | Oran | |
| | | | Astrella |
| | Noran | | |
| | | | Rissalix |
| ACHIM (imp.) | | Nerina | |
| Chestnut Stallion – 1961 | | | Risira |
| Kehailan Dajani | | | Rishan |
| AVS, AHSB Volume XII | | Radi | |
| | | | Razina |
| | Tehoura | | |
| | | | Rissam |
| | | Niseyra | |
| | | | Neraida |

Bred and exhibited by
Dr H. C. E. M. Houtappel

Imported from the Netherlands in 1971
Exported to the USA in 1984

# *Azara*

Supreme Female Champion 1973

| | | |
|---|---|---|
| | | Rissalix |
| | Blue Domino | |
| | | Niseyra |
| Manto | | |
| | | Oran |
| | Mifaria | |
| AZARA | | Rithyana |
| Chestnut Mare – 1966 | | |
| Kehaileh Dajanieh | | Manasseh |
| AHSB Volume XI | Dargee | |
| | | Myola |
| Incoronetta | | |
| | | Raseem |
| | Indian Crown | |
| | | Nisreen |

Exhibited by Mrs P. A. M. Murray
Bred by Mrs E. M. Thomas

# *Nasib*

## Junior Male Champion 1974

|  |  |  | Raktha |
|---|---|---|---|
|  |  | Indian Magic |  |
|  | Indriss |  | Indian Crown |
| NASIB |  | Rissalma | Dargee |
| Grey Colt – 1971 |  |  | Rissiletta |
| Kehailan Dajani |  |  | Irex |
| AHSB Volume XII |  | Iridos |  |
|  | Nimet |  | Rafeena |
|  |  | Indian Snowflake | Ludo |
|  |  |  | Indian Starlight |

Bred and exhibited by Mr M. A. Pitt-Rivers          Exported to Qatar in 1982

# Vonitsa

*Photonews*

Junior Female Champion 1974

| | | | |
|---|---|---|---|
| | | Argos (imp.) | Nabor |
| | Magic Argosy | | Arfa |
| | | Fairy Magic | Indian Magic |
| VONITSA | | | Farette |
| Grey Filly – 1972 | | | Raktha |
| Kehaileh Rodanieh | | Indian Magic | Indian Crown |
| AHSB Volume XII | Marinella | | Manasseh |
| | | Myolanda | Myola |

Bred and exhibited by Mrs A. M. Roberts

83

# Sheer Magic

*Photonews*

Supreme Female Champion 1974 and 1977
Mare Champion 1976

| | | | |
|---|---|---|---|
| | | | Raktha |
| | | Indian Magic | |
| | | | Indian Crown |
| | Scindian Magic | | |
| | | | Rithan |
| | | Scindia | |
| SHEER MAGIC | | | Senga |
| Grey Mare – 1967 | | | |
| Kehaileh Rodanieh | | | Rifari |
| AHSB Volume XI | | Shifari | |
| | | | Shabryeh |
| | Mafari | | |
| | | | Manasseh |
| | | Marishna | |
| | | | Rishna |

Exhibited by Mrs N. D. Hardcastle (1974)          Exported to Australia in 1978
         Mr & Mrs P. Howard Price (1977)
Bred by Mrs P. E. M. Arnold

# *Jamshid*

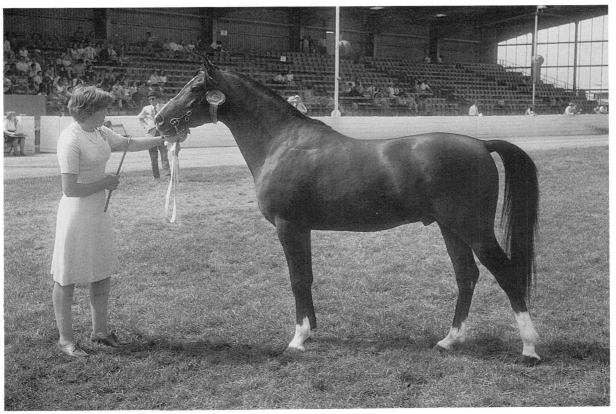

*Photonews*

## Junior Male Champion 1975

|  |  |  | Fadl |
|---|---|---|---|
|  |  | Fabah |  |
|  | The Shah (imp.) |  | Bint Bint Sabbah |
| JAMSHID |  |  | Fa Serr |
| Grey Colt – 1972 |  | Bint Fada |  |
| Seglawi Jedran |  |  | Fada |
| AHSB Volume XII |  |  | Comet |
|  |  | Grojec (imp.) |  |
|  | Balbura |  | Gastronomia |
|  |  |  | Pomeranets |
|  |  | Stopa (imp.) |  |
|  |  |  | Sofa II |

Bred and exhibited by Margaret, Lady Harmsworth Blunt

85

# *Bright Venus*

*Photonews*

Junior Female Champion 1975 and 1976
Supreme Female Champion 1976

| | | | |
|---|---|---|---|
| | | | Riffal |
| | | Oran | |
| | | | Astrella |
| | Orion | | |
| | | | Royal Diamond |
| BRIGHT VENUS | | Dancing Diamond | |
| Chestnut Mare – 1973 | | | Dancing Star |
| Kehaileh Rodanieh | | | Count Dorsaz |
| AHSB Volume XII | | Count Rapello | |
| | | | Rafeena |
| | Ghazali | | |
| | | | Raktha |
| | | Rithyana | |
| | | | Rishyana |

Bred and exhibited by Major & Mrs T. W. I. Hedley

# *Sharzar*

*Photonews*

## Supreme Male Champion 1975

| | | | |
|---|---|---|---|
| | | Star Diamond | Raktha |
| | Stargard | | Sharima |
| SHARZAR | | Somara | Nureddin II |
| Grey Stallion – 1971 | | | Silver Fire |
| Kehailan Mimri | | Blue Domino | Rissalix |
| AHSB Volume XII | | | Niseyra |
| | Sahara | Gehenna (imp.) | Doktryner |
| | | | Gazella |

Bred and exhibited by Miss C. M. Cooke

# Nahodka
*(imp.)*

## Supreme Female Champion 1975

| | | | |
|---|---|---|---|
| NAHODKA (imp.)<br>Grey Mare – 1963<br>Seglawieh Jedranieh<br>RASB, AHSB Volume XI | Knippel | Korej | Kann |
| | | | Rixalina |
| | | Parfumeria | Piolun |
| | | | Florencia |
| | Novisna | Naseem | Skowronek (imp.) |
| | | | Nasra |
| | | Niezgoda | Fetysz |
| | | | Koalicja |

Exhibited by Mrs E. Soanes
Bred by Tersk Stud, USSR

Imported from the USSR in 1966

88

# Grand Duke

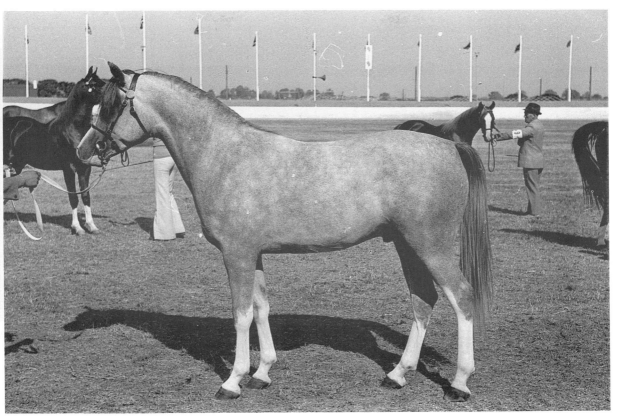

*Photonews*

Junior Male Champion 1976

| | | | |
|---|---|---|---|
| | | Indian King | Oran |
| | Crystal King | | Indian Pride |
| GRAND DUKE | | Crystal Clear | Bright Shadow |
| Grey Colt – 1974 | | | Indian Trinket |
| Kehailan Rodan | | Ludo | Blue Domino |
| AHSB Volume XIII | | | Rithyana |
| | Roxzeena | | Iran |
| | | Yaquin | Yatagan |

Exhibited by Mrs J. M. Gooding
Bred by Mr J. B. Stocks

# El Shaklan
## *(imp.)*

*Photonews*

## Junior Male Champion 1977 and 1978

| | | | |
|---|---|---|---|
| | | Morafic | Nazeer |
| | | | Mabrouka |
| | Shaker el Masri | | El Sareei |
| EL SHAKLAN (imp.) | | Zebeda | Galila |
| Grey Colt – 1975 | | | Congo |
| Family of Verana 1934 | | Tabal | Hilandera |
| (Veragua Mare) | | | Barquillo |
| VZAP, AHSB Volume XIII | Estopa | Uyaima | Imelina |

Exhibited by Major & Mrs P. W. S. Maxwell        Imported to the UK c.1977
Bred by Mrs S. Merz, Germany

*Photonews*

# *Sky Hera*

### Junior Female Champion 1977

|  |  | | Comet |
|---|---|---|---|
|  | Grojec (imp.) | | |
|  |  | | Gastronomia |
| Sky Crusader | | | |
|  |  | | Oran |
|  | Sapphire Sky | | |
| SKY HERA |  | | Nawarra (imp.) |
| Grey Filly – 1976 |  | | |
| Kehaileh Mimrieh |  | | Negatiw |
| AHSB Volume XIII | Nabor | | |
|  |  | | Lagodna |
| Gazella (i.i.u.) | | | |
|  |  | | Doktryner |
|  | Gehenna (imp.) | | |
|  |  | | Gazella |

Bred and exhibited by The Marchioness Townshend of Raynham

# *Banat*
### *(imp.)*

## Supreme Male Champion 1977

| | | | |
|---|---|---|---|
| | | Faher | Trypolis |
| | | | Ferha |
| | El Azrak | | Witraz |
| BANAT (imp.) | | Ellora | Elza |
| Bay Stallion – 1967 | | | Ofir |
| Kehailan Dueni | | Witraz | Makata |
| PASB, AHSB Volume XIII | Bandola | | Amurath Sahib |
| | | Balalajka | Iwonka III |

Exhibited by Miss P. M. Lindsay           Leased UK 1975-77
Bred by Janow Podlaski State Stud, Poland

# *Zemire*

Photo: Peter Sweet

Junior Female Champion 1978

| | | | |
|---|---|---|---|
| | | Carbine | Shammar |
| | Musketeer | | Celina (imp.) |
| ZEMIRE | | Glass Slipper | Seradin |
| Chestnut Filly – 1977 | | | Cinders |
| Seglawieh Jedranieh | | Argos (imp.) | Nabor |
| AHSB Volume XIII | | | Arfa |
| | Zarozza | Zahri | Dargee |
| | | | Zirree el Wada |

Bred and exhibited by Mrs J. R. Ratcliff

# The Shah
## *(imp.)*

*Photo: Deidre Hyde*

### Supreme Male Champion 1978

| | | | |
|---|---|---|---|
| | | Fadl | Ibn Rabdan |
| | Fabah | | Mahroussa |
| THE SHAH (imp.) | | Bint Bint Sabbah | Baiyad |
| Bay Stallion – 1966 | | | Bint Sabbah |
| Kehailan Jellabi | | Fa Serr | Fadl |
| AHRA, AHSB Volume XI | | | Bint Serra I |
| | Bint Fada | | Faddan |
| | | Fada | Aaroufa |

Exhibited by Major & Mrs T. W. I. Hedley        Imported from the USA c.1969
Bred by Henry B. Babson, USA

# *Kadidja*
## *(imp.)*

*Photo: Peter Sweet*

Supreme Female Champion 1978

|  |  |  |  |
|---|---|---|---|
|  |  |  | Ilustre |
|  |  | Sherif |  |
|  |  |  | Rebeca |
|  | Alcazar |  |  |
| KADIDJA (imp.) |  |  | Barquillo |
| Grey Mare – 1969 |  | Jacobita |  |
| Family of Verana 1934 |  |  | Ghazel Or.Ar. |
| (Veragua Mare) |  |  | Tetuan |
| SBE, AHSB Volume XIII | Chavali | Ornis |  |
|  |  |  | Fifinella |
|  |  |  | Habiente |
|  |  | Paita |  |
|  |  |  | Jaecera |

Exhibited by Dr H. C. E. M. Houtappel          Imported from Spain in 1969
Bred by Da. Maria Paz Murga, Spain

# Midnight Gold

*Photo: Peter Sweet*

Junior Male Champion 1979

| | | |
|---|---|---|
| | | Blue Domino |
| | Fari II | |
| | | Farette |
| King Cotton Gold | | |
| | | Blue Domino |
| | Dreaming Gold | |
| MIDNIGHT GOLD | | Gleaming Gold |
| Chestnut Colt – 1976 | | |
| Hamdani Simri | | Raktha |
| AHSB Volume XIII | Indian Magic | |
| | | Indian Crown |
| Enchantment | | |
| | | Dargee |
| | Dalika | |
| | | Silver Gilt |

Exhibited by Mr & Mrs J. Buchanan        Exported to Qatar in 1987
Bred by Mrs P. A. M. Murray

96

# *Najat*

*Photo: Peter Sweet*

Junior Female Champion 1979
Supreme Female Champion 1981

| | | | |
|---|---|---|---|
| | | Mikeno | Rissalix |
| | Shahid | | Namilla |
| NAJAT | | Sherrara | Grojec (imp.) |
| Grey Mare – 1976 | | | Sahirah of the Storm |
| Kehaileh Dajanieh | | Iridos | Irex |
| AHSB Volume XIII | | | Rafeena |
| | Nimet | Indian Snowflake | Ludo |
| | | | Indian Starlight |

Bred and exhibited by Mr M. A. Pitt-Rivers

# *General Gold*

Supreme Male Champion 1979

| | | | |
|---|---|---|---|
| | | Raktha | Naseem |
| | General Grant | | Razina |
| | | | Riffal |
| GENERAL GOLD | | Samsie | Naxina |
| Chestnut Stallion – 1973 | | | Rissalix |
| Kehailan Rodan | | Blue Domino | Niseyra |
| AHSB Volume XII | Golden Treasure | | Indian Gold |
| | | Gleaming Gold | Risira |

Bred and exhibited by Mrs P. A. M. Murray

# Al Shamsa

Supreme Female Champion 1979

|  |  |  | Oran |
|---|---|---|---|
|  |  | Indian King | Indian Pride |
|  | Sunlight's Allegro |  | Dargee |
| AL SHAMSA |  | Dancing Sunlight | Shades of Night |
| Chestnut Mare – 1969 |  |  | Count Dorsaz |
| Kehaileh Rodanieh |  | Count Roland | Rithyana |
| AHSB Volume XI | Roshina |  | Hassan II |
|  |  | Roshnara | Rosheiya |

Exhibited by Mrs J. Trimingham
Bred by Frances, Duchess of Rutland

# Maleik El Kheil

Photo: Peter Sweet

Junior and Supreme Male Champion 1980

|  |  |  | Morafic |
|---|---|---|---|
|  |  | Shaker el Masri | Zebeda |
|  | El Shaklan (imp.) |  | Tabal |
| MALEIK EL KHEIL |  | Estopa | Uyaima |
| Grey Colt – 1979 |  |  | Ibn Fakhri |
| Wadnan Khirsan |  | Fakhr el Kheil (imp.) | Bint Muneera |
| AHSB Volume XIV | Muneera |  | Indriss |
|  |  | Muzri | Kazra |

Bred and exhibited by
Major & Mrs P. W. S. Maxwell

Exported to the United Arab Emirates in 1992

# Zarafah

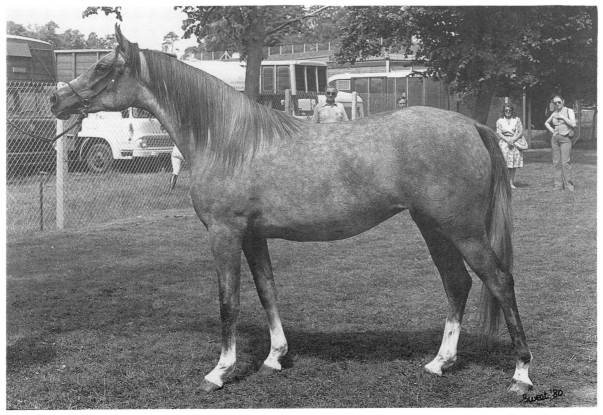

Photo: Peter Sweet

Junior and Supreme Female Champion 1980

| | | | |
|---|---|---|---|
| | | Silver Vanity | Oran |
| | Hanif | | Silver Gilt |
| ZARAFAH | | Sirella | Dargee |
| Grey Filly – 1978 | | | Shalina |
| Seglawieh Jedranieh | | Dargee | Manasseh |
| AHSB Volume XIV | | | Myola |
| | Zahri | Zirree el Wada | Naseel |
| | | | Rose Du Sable |

Bred and exhibited by Mr G. Plaister

# *Myros*

Stallion Champion 1980

MYROS
Chestnut Stallion – 1972
Wadnan Khirsan
AHSB Volume XII

| | | |
|---|---|---|
| | Indian King | Oran |
| | | Indian Pride |
| Song of India | | Silver Vanity |
| | Indira | Perle D'Or |
| | General Grant | Raktha |
| | | Samsie |
| Khamilla | | Champurrado |
| | Khamisa | Rediaa |

Exhibited by Mrs B. K. Moss
Bred by Mr & Mrs J. Lewis

# *Rishenda*

Photo: Peter Sweet

Mare Champion 1980

| | | | |
|---|---|---|---|
| | | Ludrex | Ludo |
| | | | Sirikit |
| | Donax | | Dargee |
| RISHENDA | | Dargemet | Bint Yasimet |
| Chestnut Mare – 1976 | | | Rosh |
| Kehaileh Mimrieh | | Rushti | Rufeiya |
| AHSB Volume XIII | | | |
| | Krysia | | Witraz |
| | | Karramba (imp.) | Karmen II |

Bred and exhibited by Mrs P. D. Hitchings

# *Daweish*

*Photo: Peter Sweet*

Junior and Supreme Male Champion 1981

|  |  |  | Hadban Enzahi |
|---|---|---|---|
|  |  | Mameluck | Moheba II |
|  | Melchior (imp.) |  | Ghazal |
| DAWEISH |  | Mamsahi | Masarrah |
| Grey Colt – 1978 |  |  | Irex |
| Seglawi Jedran |  | Iridos | Rafeena |
| AHSB Volume XIV | Ireena |  | Algolson |
|  |  | Cinders | Yateemah |

Bred and exhibited by Mr & Mrs J. Martin

# *Arella Bint Procyon*

*Photo: Fiona Guinness*

Junior Female Champion 1981

| | | | |
|---|---|---|---|
| | | Saludo | Maquillo |
| | Procyon (imp.) | | Jacobita |
| ARELLA BINT PROCYON | | Casiopea | Malvito |
| Grey Filly – 1980 | | | Transjordania |
| Hamdanieh Simrieh | | Sha'ir | Grojec (imp.) |
| AHSB Volume XIV | | | Sahirah of the Storm |
| | Paean of Praise | | Blue Domino |
| | | Scindigo Blue | Scindia |

Bred and exhibited by Mrs C. E. Jenkins

# *Bravado*

Photo: Peter Sweet

Stallion Champion 1981

| | | |
|---|---|---|
| | | Blue Domino |
| | Fari II | Farette |
| King Cotton Gold | | Blue Domino |
| | Dreaming Gold | Gleaming Gold |
| | | Radi |
| | Bright Shadow | Pale Shadow |
| Shindra | | Magnet |
| | Magnindra | Naxindra |

BRAVADO
Chestnut Stallion – 1976
Kehailan Dajani
AHSB Volume XIII

Exhibited by Miss F. Murray
Bred by Mrs D. M. Campbell

# Mehzeer

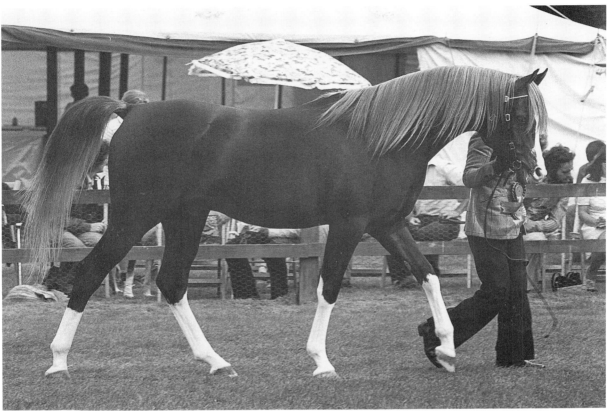

Photo: Fiona Guinness

Junior and Supreme Male Champion 1982

MEHZEER
Chestnut Colt – 1979
Wadnan Khirsan
AHSB Volume XIV

| | | | |
|---|---|---|---|
| | | Haroun | Hanif |
| | Mehriz | | Indian Snowflake |
| | | Mandahyla | Indian Magic |
| | | | Myolanda |
| | | Count Dorsaz | Rissalix |
| | Alzehra | | Shamnar |
| | | Zehraa | Irex |
| | | | Nurmana |

Bred and exhibited by Mr & Mrs D. E. Campbell

Photo: Fiona Guinness

# *Farahnaz*

## Junior and Supreme Female Champion 1982

|  |  |  |
|---|---|---|
|  | Fakhr el Kheil (imp.) | Ibn Fakhri |
|  |  | Bint Muneera |
| El Kheron |  | Indian Magic |
| FARAHNAZ | El Mabrouka |  |
| Grey Filly – 1981 |  | Muzri |
| Kehaileh Rodanieh |  | Serafix |
| AHSB Volume XIV | Royal Lancer |  |
|  |  | Maharetta |
| Naharetta (imp.) |  | Naharin |
|  | Amira Gina (imp.) |  |
|  |  | Bint Farrieh |

Bred and exhibited by Mr & Mrs R. P. Rumsey

Photo: Peter Sweet

# Silver Flame

## Stallion Champion 1982

SILVER FLAME
Grey Stallion – 1970
Kehailan Rodan
AHSB Volume XII

| | | |
|---|---|---|
| | | Raktha |
| | Indian Magic | |
| | | Indian Crown |
| Indian Flame II | | |
| | | Oran |
| | Nerinora | |
| | | Nerina |
| | | Oran |
| | Silver Vanity | |
| | | Silver Gilt |
| Silver Ripple | | |
| | | Faris |
| | Risseefa | |
| | | Risira |

Exhibited by Mrs R. Bretherton
Bred by Mr & Mrs R. G. Archer

109

# Indian Sylphette

Photo: Peter Sweet

## Mare Champion 1982

|                          |                |               |               |
|--------------------------|----------------|---------------|---------------|
|                          |                | Oran          | Riffal        |
|                          | Indian King    |               | Astrella      |
| INDIAN SYLPHETTE         |                | Indian Pride  | Irex          |
| Chestnut Mare – 1976     |                |               | Nisreen       |
| Kehaileh Dajanieh        |                | Azrak         | Blue Domino   |
| AHSB Volume XIII         | Blue Sylphide  |               | Silent Wings  |
|                          |                | Crystal Magic | Crystal Fire  |
|                          |                |               | Royal Exchange|

Bred and exhibited by Mr & Mrs W. W. Brogden

110

# Ali Al Said

*Photo: Peter Sweet*

Junior and Supreme Male Champion 1983

|  |  |  | Hadban Enzahi |
|  |  | Mameluck |  |
|  | Melchior (imp.) |  | Moheba II |
| ALI AL SAID |  |  | Ghazal |
| Grey Colt – 1982 |  | Mamsahi |  |
| Kehailan Rodan |  |  | Masarrah |
| AHSB Volume XV |  |  | Indian King |
|  |  | Sunlight's Allegro |  |
|  | Al Shamsa |  | Dancing Sunlight |
|  |  |  | Count Roland |
|  |  | Roshina |  |
|  |  |  | Roshnara |

Bred and exhibited by Mrs J. Trimingham          Exported to the USA in 1985

# Tarantara

Photo: Betty Finke

Junior and Supreme Female Champion 1983

|  |  | | Indian King |
|  |  | Crystal King | |
|  |  | | Crystal Clear |
|  | Crystal Magician | | |
|  |  | | Scindian Magic |
| TARANTARA |  | Sheer Magic | |
| Chestnut Filly – 1980 |  | | Mafari |
| Kehaileh Dajanieh |  | | Star Diamond |
| AHSB Volume XIV |  | Stargard | |
|  |  | | Somara |
|  | Selinda | | |
|  |  | | Indian King |
|  |  | Tarantella | |
|  |  | | Dancing Sunlight |

Bred and exhibited by Mr & Mrs W. W. Brogden

112

# Shodina

Photo: Peter Sweet

Mare Champion 1983

| | | | |
|---|---|---|---|
| | | The Shah (imp.) | Fabah |
| | Indian Treasure | | Bint Fada |
| | | Golden Treasure | Blue Domino |
| SHODINA | | | Gleaming Gold |
| Chestnut Mare – 1979 | | | Oran |
| Kehaileh Rodanieh | | Indian King | Indian Pride |
| AHSB Volume XIV | Delilah | | Greatheart |
| | | Esther II | Teresita |

Bred and exhibited by Mrs P. A. M. Murray

113

# Esplendor

Photo: Peter Sweet

## Junior Male Champion 1984

| | | | |
|---|---|---|---|
| | | | Tabal |
| | | Jacio | |
| | | | Teorica |
| | Ghadames (imp.) | | |
| | | | Zurich |
| ESPLENDOR | | Lopaz | |
| Bay Colt – 1983 | | | Yacaranda |
| Family of Verapaz 1935 | | | Congo |
| (Veragua Mare) | | Tabal | |
| AHSB Volume XV | Esperada (imp.) | | Hilandera |
| | | | Sherif |
| | | Berlanga | |
| | | | Teneria |

Bred and exhibited by
Major & Mrs P. W. S. Maxwell

Exported to the USSR in 1985

# *Kahramana*

Photo: Peter Sweet

## Junior Female Champion 1984

| | | | |
|---|---|---|---|
| | | Jacio | Tabal |
| | Ghadames (imp.) | | Teorica |
| | | Lopaz | Zurich |
| KAHRAMANA | | | Yacaranda |
| Chestnut Filly – 1983 | | | Indian Magic |
| Wadna Khirsanieh | | Indriss | Rissalma |
| AHSB Volume XV | Kazminda | | Mikeno |
| | | Kazra | Razehra |

Bred and exhibited by Major & Mrs P. W. S. Maxwell

# *Ralvon Elijah*
## *(imp.)*

Photo: Peter Sweet

Supreme Male Champion 1984
Senior Male Champion 1985

| | | | |
|---|---|---|---|
| | | | Talal |
| | | The Puritan | |
| | Ralvon Nazarene | | Miss Floco |
| | | | Royal Domino |
| RALVON ELIJAH (imp.) | | Trix Silver | |
| Chestnut Stallion – 1978 | | | Electricia |
| Kehailan Dajani | | | Rikham |
| AHS Aust., | | Ralvon Pilgrim | |
| AHSB Volume XIV | | | Trix Silver |
| | Mill Hill Sharmal | | |
| | | | Argent |
| | | Argency | |
| | | | Tarney |

Exhibited by Mr M. A. Pitt-Rivers           Imported from Australia in 1979
Bred by R. & V. Males, Australia              Exported to the USA in 1986

Photo: Peter Sweet

# Shahlie

### Senior Female Champion 1984

SHAHLIE
Grey Mare – 1977
Seglawieh Jedranieh
AHSB Volume XIII

| | | |
|---|---|---|
| | Haroun | Hanif |
| Shahir | | Indian Snowflake |
| | Sherrara | Grojec (imp.) |
| | | Sahirah of the Storm |
| | White Lightning | Burkan |
| White Lace | | Latawica (imp.) |
| | Nasim | Jair |
| | | Nasam |

Bred and exhibited by Mr & Mrs G. T. Greenwood

# Spearmint

Photo: Fiona Guinness

Junior Male Champion 1985

| | | | |
|---|---|---|---|
| | | Champurrado | Irex |
| | | | Niseyra |
| | Shammar | | Fedaan Or.Ar. (imp.) |
| SPEARMINT | | Somra II | Safarjal |
| Chestnut Colt – 1982 | | | Rheoboam |
| Hamdani Simri | | Blenheim | Beryl |
| AHSB Volume XV | | | |
| | Sappho | | Bahram |
| | | Selima | Siwa II |

Bred and exhibited by Mrs J. M. Oppé

118

# Spey Crystal

Photo: Peter Sweet

## Junior Female Champion 1985

| | | |
|---|---|---|
| | Crystal King | Indian King |
| | | Crystal Clear |
| Crystal Magician | | Scindian Magic |
| SPEY CRYSTAL | Sheer Magic | Mafari |
| Bay Filly – 1982 | | General Grant |
| Hamdanieh Simrieh | General Dorsaz | Azella |
| AHSB Volume XV | | Rifari |
| Farosa | Farette | Shabrette |

Exhibited by Mr G. Falconer
Bred by Mrs I. M. Bowring

# Hagunia
## (imp.)

Senior Female Champion 1985

| | | | |
|---|---|---|---|
| | | | Congo |
| | | Zancudo | |
| | | | Yaima |
| | Jabalpur | | |
| | | | Sirio IV |
| HAGUNIA (imp.) | | Ocalina | |
| Grey Mare – 1975 | | | Farina |
| Family of Verana 1934 | | | Congo |
| (Veragua Mare) | | Tabal | |
| SBE, AHSB Volume XV | Iama | | Hilandera |
| | | | Malvito |
| | | Comedia II | |
| | | | Ociosa |

Exhibited by Major & Mrs P. W. S. Maxwell        Imported from Spain in 1981
Bred by D. Alfredo Erquicia Aranda, Spain

# *Kuraishi*

Photo: Peter Sweet

## Junior Male Champion 1986

KURAISHI
Grey Colt – 1983
Wadnan Khirsan
AHSB Volume XV

| | | |
|---|---|---|
| | | Shaker el Masri |
| | El Shaklan (imp.) | |
| | | Estopa |
| Maleik el Kheil | | |
| | | Fakhr el Kheil (imp.) |
| | Muneera | |
| | | Muzri |
| | | Morafic |
| | Shakhs (imp.) | |
| | | Shiaa |
| Kazra el Saghira | | |
| | | Mikeno |
| | Kazra | |
| | | Zehraa |

Exhibited by Mrs B. D. Elliott & Miss J. P. Round
Bred by Major & Mrs P. W. S. Maxwell

Photo: Peter Sweet

# *Riazana*

## Junior Female Champion 1986

| | | | |
|---|---|---|---|
| | | Darjeel | Dargee |
| | Riaz | | Rajjela |
| RIAZANA | | Razehra | Rashid |
| Chestnut Filly – 1984 | | | Zehraa |
| Wadna Khirsanieh | | Al Malik | Marino Marini |
| AHSB Volume XV | | | Bright Gleam |
| | Zaian | Zehraa | Irex |
| | | | Nurmana |

Bred and exhibited by Mrs J. Trimingham

# *Triumphal Chant*

Photo: Peter Sweet

Senior Male Champion 1986

| | | | |
|---|---|---|---|
| | | El Azrak | Faher |
| | Banat (imp.) | | Ellora |
| TRIUMPHAL CHANT | | Bandola | Witraz |
| Bay Stallion – 1976 | | | Balalajka |
| Hamdani Simri | | Sha'ir | Grojec (imp.) |
| AHSB Volume XIII | | | Sahirah of the Storm |
| | Paean of Praise | Scindigo Blue | Blue Domino |
| | | | Scindia |

Exhibited by Misses J. R. & F. Van Lennep
Bred by Mrs N. D. Hardcastle

# Bint Ludoet
## *(imp.)*

Photo: Peter Sweet

Senior Female Champion 1986

|  |  | Dargee | Manasseh |
|  |  |  | Myola |
|  | Darjeel |  |  |
|  |  | Rajjela | Grand Royal |
| BINT LUDOET (imp.) |  |  | Nuhajjela |
| Chestnut Mare – 1979 |  |  |  |
| Kehailet Ajuz |  | Ludo | Blue Domino |
| SBC BA, |  |  | Rithyana |
| AHSB Volume XVI | Ludoet |  |  |
|  |  | Dargemet | Dargee |
|  |  |  | Bint Yasimet |

Exhibited by Mrs E. Maes-Jones          Imported from Belgium in 1985
Bred by Mrs E. K. Jones

# *Estasan Ibn Estopa*
## *(imp.)*

Photo: Betty Finke

Junior Male Champion 1987

| | | | |
|---|---|---|---|
| **ESTASAN IBN ESTOPA (imp.)**<br>Grey Colt – 1984<br>Family of Verana 1934<br>(Veragua Mare)<br>VZAP, AHSB Volume XVI | Ibn Estopa (imp.) | Shaker el Masri | Morafic |
| | | | Zebeda |
| | | Estopa | Tabal |
| | | | Uyaima |
| | Bint Estawa | Malik | Hadban Enzahi |
| | | | Malikah |
| | | Estawa | Shaker el Masri |
| | | | Estopa |

Exhibited by Mr & Mrs B. D. Blake          Imported from Germany in 1985
Bred by Gestut Om El Arab, Germany

125

# *Fazleta*

Junior Female Champion 1987

| | | | |
|---|---|---|---|
| | | Gai Parada | Ferzon |
| | Gai Gaspacho (imp.) | | Azleta |
| FAZLETA | | Gai Grise | Ferzon |
| Grey Filly – 1985 | | | Gavrelle |
| Hamdanieh Simrieh | | Crystal Magician | Crystal King |
| AHSB Volume XV | | | Sheer Magic |
| | Crystal Farifi | Farosa | General Dorsaz |
| | | | Farette |

Exhibited by Mr P. Gamlin
Bred by Mrs I. M. Bowring

# Manich
## (imp.)

### Senior Male Champion 1987

| | | |
|---|---|---|
| | | Amurath Sahib |
| | Arax | |
| Nabeg | | Angara |
| | | Naseem |
| | Nomenklatura | |
| | | Mammona |
| | | Negatiw |
| | Salon | |
| Miest | | Sonata |
| | | Priboj |
| | Metropolia | |
| | | Mammona |

MANICH (imp.)
Grey Stallion – 1975
Kehailan Mimri
RASB, AHSB Volume XVI

Exhibited by Mrs J. R. Ratcliff
Bred by Tersk Stud, USSR

Imported from Italy in 1986
Exported to Italy in 1989

# Sianah Gold

Senior Female Champion 1987

| SIANAH GOLD | | | |
|---|---|---|---|
| | | Benjamin | Champurrado |
| | St. Simon | | Baranova |
| | | Sabrina | Rheoboam |
| | | | Sesame |
| | | Fari II | Blue Domino |
| | Autumn Gold | | Farette |
| | | Gleaming Gold | Indian Gold |
| | | | Risira |

SIANAH GOLD
Chestnut Mare – 1978
Seglawieh Jedranieh
AHSB Volume XIV

Bred and exhibited by Mrs P. A. M. Murray

# *Saker*

Junior Male Champion 1988

|  |  |  | Ludo |
|---|---|---|---|
|  |  | Ludomino | Yemama |
|  | Ahmoun |  | Mikeno |
| SAKER |  | Shtaura | Safara |
| Grey Colt – 1985 |  |  | Indian King |
| Kehailan Dajani |  | Dancing King | Dancing Sunlight |
| AHSB Volume XV |  |  | Ludo |
|  | Moulton Star | Indian Astra | Indian Starlight |

Exhibited by Miss E. Brehaut
Bred by Mrs J. D. Ferguson

# *Razilka*

Photo: Peter Sweet

Junior Female Champion 1988

|  |  |  | Celebes |
|  |  | Rezus |  |
|  |  |  | Rezeda |
|  | Rezolute Bay (imp.) |  |  |
|  |  |  | Tornado |
| RAZILKA |  | Mystical Lady |  |
| Chestnut Filly – 1985 |  |  | Silver Mistique |
| Hamdanieh Simrieh |  |  | Greatheart |
| AHSB Volume XV |  | Marania Gold |  |
|  | Rachinka |  | Dreaming Gold |
|  |  |  | Hanif |
|  |  | Silver Rani |  |
|  |  |  | Silver Grey |

Bred and exhibited by Mrs R. R. Carr

# Shahpoor

Photo: SAPS

## Senior Male Champion 1988

| | | | |
|---|---|---|---|
| | | Fabah | Fadl |
| | The Shah (imp.) | | Bint Bint Sabbah |
| SHAHPOOR | | Bint Fada | Fa Serr |
| Bay Stallion – 1971 | | | Fada |
| Kehailan Rodan | | Mikeno | Rissalix |
| AHSB Volume XII | Mikoletta | | Namilla |
| | | Myoletta | Manasseh |
| | | | Myola |

Exhibited by Mr & Mrs E. Jones
Bred by Capt. & Mrs M. R. Biggs

131

# *Faery Rose*

Senior Female Champion 1988

| | | | Bask |
|---|---|---|---|
| | | Tornado | |
| | Silver Scenario | | Silwara |
| | (imp.) | | Nabor |
| FAERY ROSE | | Countess Nabor | |
| Chestnut Mare – 1984 | | | Delilah |
| Seglawieh Jedranieh | | | Rushti |
| AHSB Volume XV | | Kossak | |
| | Faery Snow | | Karramba (imp.) |
| | | | Sudeir |
| | | Susannah | |
| | | | Ghayran |

Bred and exhibited by Mrs C. Plaistowe

# Ibn Warsaw

Photo: Betty Finke

Junior Male Champion 1989

| | | Ferneyn |
|---|---|---|
| | Ferzon | |
| Gai Warsaw (imp.) | | Fersara |
| | | Comet |
| | Paleta | |
| | | Planeta |
| | | Mameluck |
| | Melchior (imp.) | |
| | | Mamsahi |
| Princess Melchia | | Gold Rex |
| | Radwanah | |
| | | Indian Rain |

IBN WARSAW
Grey Colt – 1987
Kehailan Rodan
AHSB Volume XVI

Bred and exhibited by Mrs J. Trimingham

# Zircon Karisma

Photo: C. Massey

Junior Female Champion 1989

| | | | |
|---|---|---|---|
| | | Ludrex | Ludo |
| | Donax | | Sirikit |
| ZIRCON KARISMA | | Dargemet | Dargee |
| Bay Filly – 1988 | | | Bint Yasimet |
| Kehaileh Mimrieh | | Rushti | Rosh |
| AHSB Volume XVI | | | Rufeiya |
| | Krysia | Karramba (imp.) | Witraz |
| | | | Karmen II |

Bred and exhibited by Mrs P. D. Hitchings

134

# Esta-Espashan
## *(imp.)*

Photo: Fiona Guinness

## Senior Male Champion 1989

| | | | Hadban Enzahi |
|---|---|---|---|
| | | Malik | |
| | Ibn Estasha | | Malikah |
| | | | Shaker el Masri |
| ESTA-ESPASHAN (imp.) | | Estasha | |
| Grey Stallion – 1983 | | | Estopa |
| Seglawi Jedran | | | Dardir |
| AVS, AHSB Volume XVI | | Saudi | |
| | Sadika | | Sake |
| | | | Exelsjor |
| | | Scheherazade | |
| | | | Lalage |

Exhibited by Mr I. Needham          Imported from the Netherlands in 1988
Bred by G. C. Van Dooren, the Netherlands

# *Harida*

Senior Female Champion 1989

| | | | Silver Vanity |
|---|---|---|---|
| | | Hanif | |
| | | | Sirella |
| | Haroun | | |
| | | | Ludo |
| HARIDA | | Indian Snowflake | |
| Grey Mare – 1973 | | | Indian Starlight |
| Kehailet Ajuz | | | Irex |
| AHSB Volume XII | | Iridos | |
| | | | Rafeena |
| | Armida | | |
| | | | Amurath Sahib |
| | | Arwila (imp.) | |
| | | | Wilga |

Exhibited by Mrs C. A. Rone-Clarke
Bred by Mr I. W. Denman

# Platoon "HT"
### (imp.)

Junior Male Champion 1990

| | | | |
|---|---|---|---|
| | | Gondolier | Palas |
| | Pedant | | Gonagra |
| | | Pentoda | Bandos |
| PLATOON "HT" (imp.) | | | Piewica |
| Grey Colt – 1987 | | Sedan | Comet |
| Family of Szamrajowka | | | Salwa |
| AHSB Volume XVII | Padan | | Aswan |
| | | Pandora | Peschinka |

Exhibited by Mrs C. Watts       Imported from the Netherlands in 1990
Bred by Prof. & Mrs W. A. Moonen, the Netherlands

137

Photo: Pleasure Prints (Area '...

# *Aureme*

### Junior Female Champion 1990

| AUREME<br>Chestnut Filly – 1989<br>Kehaileh Rodanieh<br>AHSB Volume XVI | Aurelian | Ben Rabba (imp.) | Aurab |
| --- | --- | --- | --- |
| | | | Rollicka |
| | | Estrella | Halma |
| | | | Rexbaya |
| | Azeme Bint Gleam | Silver Flame | Indian Flame II |
| | | | Silver Ripple |
| | | Bright Gleam | Aldourie |
| | | | Pale Shadow |

Exhibited by Mrs G. M. Lancaster
Bred by Mrs P. N. Kirch

# Pandoer "HT"
## *(imp.)*

Senior Male Champion 1990

| | | | |
|---|---|---|---|
| | | | Negatiw |
| | | Gon | |
| | | | Gomora |
| | Pentagon | | |
| | | | Aswan |
| | | Pandora | |
| PANDOER "HT" (imp.) | | | Peschinka |
| Grey Stallion – 1981 | | | |
| Family of Szamrajowka | | | Comet |
| AHSB Volume XVII | | Sedan | |
| | | | Salwa |
| | Padan | | |
| | | | Aswan |
| | | Pandora | |
| | | | Peschinka |

Exhibited by Mrs N. Howard Price          Imported from the Netherlands in 1990
Bred by Prof. & Mrs W. A. Moonen, the Netherlands

# *Grey Wood Nymph*

Photo: Peter Sweet

Senior Female Champion 1990

GREY WOOD NYMPH
Grey Mare – 1983
Kehaileh Rodanieh
AHSB Volume XV

| | | |
|---|---|---|
| | | Count Roland |
| | Roxan | |
| | | Bint Roxana |
| The Prince of Orange | | |
| | | Zehros |
| | Corn Marigold | |
| | | Schima |
| | | Nabor |
| | Argos (imp.) | |
| | | Arfa |
| Holly Blue | | |
| | | Blue Domino |
| | Sapphire Blue | |
| | | Risanira |

Bred and exhibited by Mr M. Harris

# Nayef

Photo: Pleasure Prints (Area 'D')

## Junior Male Champion 1991

| | | Salon |
|---|---|---|
| | Moment | Malpia |
| Narim RASB | | Nabeg |
| (imp.) | Nejnaia | Nariadnai |
| NAYEF | | Tornado |
| Grey Colt – 1988 | Silver Scenario (imp.) | Countess Naborr |
| Hamdani Simri | | Plakat |
| AHSB Volume XVI | | |
| | Bint Nevidal | |
| | Nevidal (imp.) | Nasturcia |

Exhibited by Mr P. Gamlin
Bred by Mrs H. J. Kadri

# Zucasja

## Junior Female Champion 1991

|  |  |  | Eleuzis |
|---|---|---|---|
|  |  | Partner | Parma |
|  | Rumak (imp.) |  | Exelsjor |
| ZUCASJA |  | Rucasja | Rusznica |
| Grey Filly – 1989 |  |  | Diamond Star |
| Seglawieh Jedranieh |  | Aboud | Azeme Bint Gleam |
| AHSB Volume XVII |  |  | Musketeer |
|  | Zabelia | Zohar | Zarozza |

Bred and exhibited by Mrs G. M. Lancaster

# *Mustaphah*

Photo: Peter Sweet

## Senior Male Champion 1991

| | | | |
|---|---|---|---|
| MUSTAPHAH<br>Grey Stallion – 1978<br>Seglawi Jedran<br>AHSB Volume XIV | Melchior (imp.) | Mameluck | Hadban Enzahi |
| | | | Moheba II |
| | | Mamsahi | Ghazal |
| | | | Masarrah |
| | Crystal Shadow | Bey Shadow | Bright Shadow |
| | | | Farette |
| | | Nasim | Jair |
| | | | Nasam |

Exhibited by Mrs P. Harrison
Bred by Mrs A. Potts

# *Aliha*

*Photo: Peter Sweet*

Senior Female Champion 1991

| | | | Raktha |
|---|---|---|---|
| | | Indian Magic | |
| | | | Indian Crown |
| | Indian Silver | | |
| | | | Dargee |
| ALIHA | | Dalika | |
| Grey Mare – 1977 | | | Silver Gilt |
| Kehaileh Jellabieh | | | Nazeer |
| AHSB Volume XIII | | Ansata Ibn Halima | |
| | | | Halima |
| | AK Atallah (imp.) | | |
| | | | Ibn Moniet el Nefous |
| | | Al Nahr Mon Ami | |
| | | | Bint Fada |

Bred and exhibited by          Exported to the USA in 1985 and reimported
Major & Mrs P. W. S. Maxwell

# Crusader
## *(imp.)*

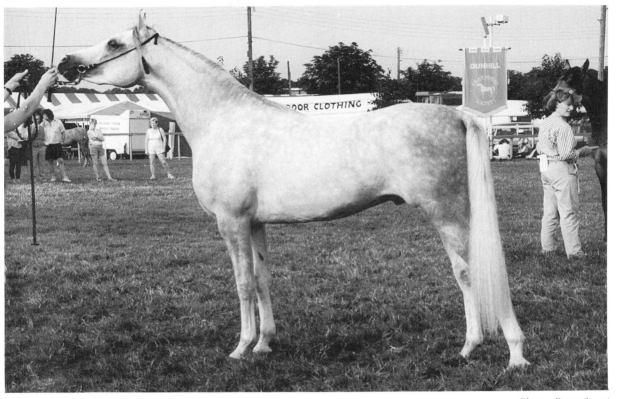

Photo: Peter Sweet

## Junior Male Champion 1992

|  |  |  |
|---|---|---|
|  |  | Ibn Halima |
|  | Ansata Halim Shah | |
|  |  | Ansata Rosetta |
| Salaa el Dine | | |
|  |  | Alaa El Din |
|  | Hanan | |
|  |  | Mona |

CRUSADER (imp.)
Grey Colt – 1990
Family of Samrae
FA, AHSB Vol. XVII

|  |  |  |
|---|---|---|
|  |  | Ibn Moniet el Nefous |
|  | Na Ibn Moniet | |
|  |  | Roufah |
| AK Kastana | | |
|  |  | Morafic |
|  | Nadafi | |
|  |  | Sammara |

Exhibited by Major & Mrs P. W. S. Maxwell
Bred by Countess Lewenhaupt, Sweden

Imported from Sweden in 1990

145

# TAS Fascination

Photo: Pleasure Prints (Area 'D')

Junior Female Champion 1992

|  |  |  | Ludrex |
|  |  | Donax |  |
|  |  |  | Dargemet |
|  | Zircon Nazeer |  |  |
|  |  |  | Saab (imp.) |
| TAS FASCINATION |  | Kazaba |  |
| Grey Filly – 1991 |  |  | Kazamah |
| Family of Kadranka |  |  | White Lightning |
| AHSB Volume XVII |  | Carmargue |  |
|  |  |  | Velvet Shadow |
|  | Jemille |  |  |
|  |  |  | Makor (imp.) |
|  |  | Bint Jamiellah |  |
|  |  |  | Aphrodite (imp.) |

Exhibited by Mrs P. D. Hitchings
Bred by Tudor Arabian Stud

146

Photo: Kan

# Bespechni
### (imp.)

## Senior Male Champion 1992

| | | | |
|---|---|---|---|
| | | | Mak |
| | | Kumir | |
| | | | Kapella |
| | Pakistan | | |
| | | | Aswan |
| | | Panagia | |
| BESPECHNI (imp.) | | | Pustinia |
| Grey Stallion – 1987 | | | |
| Kehailan Moradi | | | Aswan |
| RASB, AHSB Volume XVII | | Mashuk | |
| | | | Malutka |
| | Bionika | | |
| | | | Arax |
| | | Naturshitsa | |
| | | | Neposeda |

Exhibited by Sheikh Abdullah Bin Khalifa Al Thani
Bred by Tersk Stud, USSR

Imported from the
Netherlands in 1991

# Pilarka
## *(imp.)*

Photo: Betty Finke

## Senior Female Champion 1992

|  |  |  |  |
|---|---|---|---|
|  |  | Aswan | Nazeer |
|  |  |  | Yosreia |
|  | Palas |  |  |
| PILARKA (imp.) |  | Panel | Nil |
| Grey Mare – 1975 |  |  | Platina |
| Family of Szamrajowka |  | Negatiw | Naseem |
| PASB, AHRA, |  |  |  |
| AHSB Volume XVII | Pierzga |  | Taraszcza |
|  |  | Piewica | Priboj |
|  |  |  | Wlodarka |

Exhibited by Mr P. Gucci

Bred by Janow Podlaski State Stud, Poland

Imported from the USA in 1992

# INDEX OF CHAMPIONS
## ARRANGED ALPHABETICALLY

| Name | Year | Championship | Page |
|------|------|--------------|------|
| DARJEEL | 1965 | Junior Male | 56 |
| | 1968 | Supreme Male | " |
| | 1969 | Supreme Male | " |
| | 1970 | Supreme Male | " |
| DAWEISH | 1981 | Junior Male | 104 |
| | 1981 | Supreme Male | " |
| DOMATELLA | 1971 | Supreme Female | 74 |
| ELARA | 1965 | Junior Female | 57 |
| EL MELUK | 1966 | Supreme Male | 60 |
| | 1967 | Supreme Male | " |
| ELOIA | 1960 | Supreme Female | 44 |
| EL SANTO | 1970 | Junior Male | 69 |
| EL SHAKLAN | 1977 | Junior Male | 90 |
| | 1978 | Junior Male | " |
| ESPLENDOR | 1984 | Junior Male | 114 |
| ESTA-ESPASHAN | 1989 | Senior Male | 135 |
| ESTASAN IBN ESTOPA | 1987 | Junior Male | 125 |
| FAERY ROSE | 1988 | Senior Female | 132 |
| FARAHNAZ | 1982 | Junior Female | 108 |
| | 1982 | Supreme Female | " |
| FAZLETA | 1987 | Junior Female | 126 |
| GENERAL GOLD | 1979 | Supreme Male | 98 |
| GHAZALI | 1972 | Supreme Female | 77 |
| GOLDEN DOMINO | 1963 | Junior Male | 50 |
| GRAND DUKE | 1976 | Junior Male | 89 |
| GRAND ROYAL | 1953 | Supreme Male | 21 |
| | 1956 | Supreme Male | " |
| GREY WOOD NYMPH | 1990 | Senior Female | 140 |
| HAGUNIA | 1985 | Senior Female | 120 |
| HARIDA | 1989 | Senior Female | 136 |
| HAROUN | 1971 | Junior Male | 71 |
| | 1972 | Stallion | " |
| | 1974 | Supreme Male | " |
| IBN WARSAW | 1989 | Junior Male | 133 |
| INDIAN MAGIC | 1957 | Supreme Male | 34 |
| INDIAN SYLPHETTE | 1982 | Mare | 110 |
| JAMSHID | 1975 | Junior Male | 85 |
| KADIDJA | 1978 | Supreme Female | 95 |
| KAHRAMANA | 1984 | Junior Female | 115 |
| KAMI | 1960 | Junior Male | 42 |
| KING COTTON GOLD | 1972 | Junior Male | 75 |
| | 1972 | Supreme Male | " |
| KURAISHI | 1986 | Junior Male | 121 |
| LYVIA | 1966 | Junior Female | 59 |

| Name | Year | Championship | Page |
|---|---|---|---|
| SHEER MAGIC (cont.) | 1976 | Mare | 84 |
| | 1977 | Supreme Female | " |
| SHERIFA | 1957 | Supreme Female | 35 |
| SHODINA | 1983 | Mare | 113 |
| SIANAH GOLD | 1987 | Supreme Female | 128 |
| SILENT WINGS | 1957 | Junior Female | 33 |
| SILVER FLAME | 1982 | Stallion | 109 |
| SILVER GREY | 1960 | Junior Female | 43 |
| | 1963 | Supreme Female | " |
| | 1965 | Supreme Female | " |
| SILVER SHADOW | 1953 | Supreme Female | 22 |
| SILVER SHEEN | 1963 | Junior Female | 52/53 |
| | 1964 | Junior Female | " |
| | 1964 | Supreme Female | " |
| | 1968 | Supreme Female | " |
| | 1969 | Supreme Female | " |
| | 1970 | Supreme Female | " |
| SILVER VANITY | 1958 | Supreme Male | 38 |
| | 1962 | Supreme Male | " |
| SIRELLA | 1956 | Junior Female | 30/31 |
| | 1956 | Supreme Female | " |
| | 1959 | Supreme Female | " |
| | 1962 | Supreme Female | " |
| SKY HERA | 1977 | Junior Female | 91 |
| SPEARMINT | 1985 | Junior Male | 118 |
| SPEY CRYSTAL | 1985 | Junior Female | 119 |
| SUGAR PLUM FAIRY | 1966 | Supreme Female | 61 |
| SUNLIGHT'S ALLEGRO | 1966 | Junior Male | 58 |
| TARANTARA | 1983 | Junior Female | 112 |
| | 1983 | Supreme Female | " |
| TAS FASCINATION | 1992 | Junior Female | 146 |
| TERESITA | 1954 | Junior Female | 24 |
| | 1954 | Supreme Female | " |
| THE SHAH | 1978 | Supreme Male | 94 |
| TRIUMPHAL CHANT | 1986 | Supreme Male | 123 |
| VONITSA | 1974 | Junior Female | 83 |
| YEMAMA | 1962 | Junior Female | 49 |
| ZARAFAH | 1980 | Junior Female | 101 |
| | 1980 | Supreme Female | " |
| ZEMIRE | 1978 | Junior Female | 93 |
| ZIRCON KARISMA | 1989 | Junior Female | 134 |
| ZUCASJA | 1991 | Junior Female | 142 |